T0361287

Cambridge Elements

Elements in Epistemology
edited by
Stephen Hetherington
University of New South Wales, Sydney

STRATIFIED VIRTUE EPISTEMOLOGY

A Defence

J. Adam Carter
University of Glasgow

CAMBRIDGE
UNIVERSITY PRESS

CAMBRIDGE
UNIVERSITY PRESS

Shaftesbury Road, Cambridge CB2 8EA, United Kingdom

One Liberty Plaza, 20th Floor, New York, NY 10006, USA

477 Williamstown Road, Port Melbourne, VIC 3207, Australia

314–321, 3rd Floor, Plot 3, Splendor Forum, Jasola District Centre,
New Delhi – 110025, India

103 Penang Road, #05–06/07, Visioncrest Commercial, Singapore 238467

Cambridge University Press is part of Cambridge University Press & Assessment,
a department of the University of Cambridge.

We share the University's mission to contribute to society through the pursuit of
education, learning and research at the highest international levels of excellence.

www.cambridge.org
Information on this title: www.cambridge.org/9781009468268

DOI: 10.1017/9781009067546

© J. Adam Carter 2023

First published 2023

A catalogue record for this publication is available from the British Library.

ISBN 978-1-009-46826-8 Hardback
ISBN 978-1-009-06619-8 Paperback
ISSN 2398-0567 (online)
ISSN 2514-3832 (print)

Stratified Virtue Epistemology

A Defence

Elements in Epistemology

DOI: 10.1017/9781009067546
First published online: December 2023

J. Adam Carter
University of Glasgow
Author for correspondence: J. Adam Carter, adam.carter@glasgow.ac.uk

Abstract: This accessible Element defends a version of virtue epistemology shown to have all-things-considered advantages over other views on the market. The view is unorthodox, in that it incorporates Sosa's animal/reflective knowledge distinction, which has thus far had few takers. The author shows why embracing a multi-tiered framework is not a liability within virtue epistemology but instead affords it an edge not attainable otherwise. The particular account of knowledge goes beyond Sosa's own view by introducing and incorporating several theoretical innovations (regarding both basing and risk, as well as the introduction of multiple species of reflective knowledge) that are aimed at revamping how we think about 'high-grade' knowledge, how we attain it, and what it demands of us. The result is a new and improved stratified virtue epistemology that can hold up against scrutiny.

Keywords: virtue epistemology, Sosa, performance normativity, epistemic competence, cognitive achievement

ISBNs: 9781009468268 (HB), 9781009066198 (PB), 9781009067546 (OC)
ISSNs: 2398-0567 (online), 2514-3832 (print)

Contents

Preface

This Element defends a 'stratified' version of virtue epistemology. Virtue epistemology is built around a simple idea: knowing a fact essentially involves believing it truly through the exercise of ability; knowledge is thus always and everywhere an *achievement* on the part of the knower. This simple idea is theoretically powerful. Section 1 shows that, working with just this simple 'knowledge = truth through ability' slogan, we can get *far* better results in epistemology – demonstrated across a spectrum of theoretical test points and cases – than critics of virtue epistemology have appreciated thus far. And it is shown to do better than notable competitor proposals, such as safety-based accounts of knowledge. But as we'll see, there is, at the end of the day, only so far you can get with just one *level* of knowledge. Some residual problems remain, no matter what moves one tries to make while working with a single, 'uni-level' virtue epistemology.

Against this background, Section 2 follows Ernest Sosa's lead and considers what we can achieve by adding a second 'level' to our virtue-theoretic picture – a distinction between *animal* and *reflective* knowledge (roughly: between knowing, and knowing that you know – viz., knowing *knowledgeably*). It is shown how a multi-tiered, 'stratified' version of virtue epistemology gets better results, all things considered, than a more traditional, 'uni-level' virtue epistemology, and with fewer theoretical costs. In the course of developing this multi-level idea, Section 2 takes us beyond Sosa and offers a new account of reflective knowledge – carving out a place for both *descriptive* and *predictive* reflective knowledge, and the distinct theoretical roles each plays.

Section 3 then shows how the account – which by this point recognises a stratified picture of *knowledge* – is improved further yet through the introduction of *stratified beliefs* into the picture; on this view, (put roughly) some beliefs *constitutively aim* higher, epistemically speaking, than others. Working with this idea, Section 3 then develops a new account of the highest grade of knowledge – fully apt judgement – which (motivated along the way by several critiques of Sosa's account) incorporates theoretical innovations concerning both (i) *level-connecting* (between the animal and reflective levels), and (ii) how it is that 'high grade' knowledge interfaces with epistemic risk and background beliefs that we can non-negligently take for granted.

The resulting picture is a new and improved version of virtue epistemology, one that is situated broadly within the Sosan tradition, but which takes us beyond it in important new ways. I'm grateful to Stephen Hetherington – series editor for Cambridge University Press's *Epistemology Elements* series – for encouraging me to write this Element for the series, and to two helpful anonymous referees at Cambridge University Press and to Stephen – for helpful feedback. This research has received funding from the European Research Council (ERC) under the European Union's Horizon 2020 research and innovation programme (grant agreement No 948356, KnowledgeLab project, PI: Mona Simion). Thanks also to the Leverhulme Trust (RPG-2019-302) and the AHRC (AH/W005077/1) and (AH/W008424/1) for supporting this research.

1 Virtue Epistemology: One Level Is Good

The core knowledge thesis embraced by virtue epistemologists is that that propositional knowledge is type-identical with *apt* belief – viz., belief whose correctness is because of ability. The devil is in the details of the view (which we'll jump right into in this section), but the basic idea is just as simple as it sounds: some of your true beliefs are due to luck; those aren't knowledge. Those that are due to ability (and only those) are the ones you know. That's the crux of the idea. Can a theory of knowledge so simple be extensionally adequate?

If you've done a bit of epistemology already, you might think not. There are some well-known lines of argument in the literature that hold that apt belief is neither necessary nor sufficient for knowing.[1] Moreover, there are sceptics about the very project of analysing knowledge.[2] But we'll see that the situation turns out to be much better than critics have appreciated. This section is going to show just how well the simple idea that knowledge is apt belief can do, without any extra bells, whistles, or (as we'll add in later sections) 'levels'.

The plan for this opening section will be to begin by showing how the knowledge = apt belief equivalence allies itself naturally with two related theses to form a kind of 'core triad'. The core triad, we'll see, holds up really well against the competition once we test its explanatory power across a relatively wide testing ground of cases and problems. Along the way we'll distinguish two substantive ways of characterising the template idea that knowledge is apt belief – due to John Greco and Ernest Sosa, respectively. The idea that knowledge = Greco-aptness does well, but we'll see the idea that knowledge = Sosa-aptness does even better (and both do better in our testing ground than notable competition, including Pritchard's anti-luck virtue epistemology). Methodologically, we'll keep a kind of running scoreboard throughout the section, with a final scoreboard at the end. The final scoreboard – while it shows just how well the 'knowledge = Sosa-aptness' view performs – also leaves us with some lingering questions, which will set the scene for the next section, where we begin to see advantages of a multi-tiered account of knowledge.

---

[1] See, for example, Lackey 2007; Pritchard 2012.   [2] See the Appendix to Section 1.

1.1 The Basic Core Triad

The very idea that knowledge is type-identical with apt belief already – and before we get into different substantive glosses – commits its defenders to two closely related theses. First, consider that *aptness* – a property a belief has when its success is because of ability – is a *normative* assessment: by calling a belief apt we evaluate the belief relative to an implicit standard governing the kind of attempt a belief is. From the core idea that knowledge is type-identical with apt belief, we are tacitly signed on to the thesis that knowledge is a *normative* kind, as opposed to (say) a natural kind.[3] Second, when any aim (an archery shot, a dance performance, etc.) is secured not just luckily but through skill or ability, the success is *thereby* an *achievement*, where (pre-theoretically at least) we take the (attributive) goodness of an achievement to outstrip the goodness of the mere success. Qua achievement, then, knowledge is not merely normative, but it also has some (defeasible[4]) normative 'oomph'.

With these ideas in play, we can now see that the core idea that knowledge is apt belief (viz., the virtue epistemologists's core knowledge thesis (CKT)) is best understood as the 'core' of a key triad of claims, all three of which are capable of doing explanatory work.

Core Triad (Virtue Epistemology)
- **Core knowledge thesis (CKT)**: Propositional knowledge is apt belief.
- **Normative kind thesis (NKT)**: Knowledge is a normative kind.
- **Cognitive achievement thesis (CAT)**: Knowledge is a (species of) cognitive achievement.

This package is often, *by default*, endorsed by those who accept also the orthodox 'uni-level' thesis about grades or levels of knowledge:

- **Uni-level thesis**: There is one and only one grade of propositional knowledge.

For the virtue epistemologist, then, the uni-level thesis implies a commitment to thinking that knowledge-qua-apt belief is a *single normative kind*, and that the achievement one attains when knowing is always and everywhere just the achievement that is associated with the normative kind of *apt belief.*

---

[3] Normative kinds, unlike natural kinds, are type-individuated in an irreducibly normative way. Social kinds might be either normative or natural kinds, though there is disagreement on this point (Bird and Tobin 2022, section 2.4).

[4] An achievement's being trivial or evil might implicate that it is all-things-considered of little (or bad) worth. See, for example, Carter 2023; Sosa 2021, chapter 2.

But what exactly does apt belief involve, in virtue of requiring the belief be a kind of 'success from ability'? Let's now think about one popular answer to this question.

1.2 Knowledge as Greco-Aptness

One prominent defence of the core triad – paired with the uni-level thesis – is due to John Greco (2010), whose book *Achieving Knowledge* is centred around the simple slogan that knowledge is always and everywhere *success from ability*.

To put some substantive meat on the bones, we need to know precisely what Greco means by both 'ability' and by 'attributable to'. He offers his own distinctive account of both. *Cognitive abilities*, for Greco, are *environment relative* stable dispositions to believe truly reliably. For example, you might right now have a visual-perceptual ability that you exercise to correctly ascertain the colour of the wall in the room, but for Greco you wouldn't possess or exercise this ability if you entered a house of illusions, where visual perception is unreliable.

Regarding *attributability*: For Greco, a belief's correctness is *attributable* to ability when ability (rather than, for example, luck) is the *most salient part of a causal explanation for why the subject believed truly.*[5] Greco's particular way of defending CKT, then, involves the following substantive view of what aptness involves; for convenience, call this *Greco-aptness*:

> **Greco-aptness** A subject's *S*'s belief that *p* is apt iff the most salient part of a causal explanation for why *S*'s belief that *p* is true is *S*'s (environment-relative) stable disposition to believe truly.

By identifying knowledge with Greco-aptness, Greco holds that the kind of *achievement* one has when knowing is one that requires their environment-relative abilities to most saliently (alternatively: primarily) causally explain why their belief is correct. If something else (luck, a special helper, etc.) is comparatively more salient as part of a causal explanation for why they got it right, or if one's environment-relative abilities partially but don't *primarily* explain why they got it right, then their success is not a cognitive achievement; their belief is not apt, and they fail to know.

---

[5] This is a standard simplification of Greco's 2003–10 view, which we find in, for example, works by Pritchard (2012) and Lackey (2007). One reason for opting for this simplification in presentation is that Greco takes the mechanisms governing salience to support picking '*one* partial cause rather than another' which is 'important' within a wider causal explanation (see Greco 2010, 74). Greco's position takes a different shape in another work (Greco 2020b). Given the attention the earlier view has received, combined with limited space, this Element will focus on the 2003–10 view.

1.3 Greco-Aptness and Gettier

Perhaps the most impressive advertisement for Greco's identification of knowledge with Greco-aptness is the way his view easily 'rules out' standard Gettier cases as cases of knowledge. To see how this works, just consider the following simple Gettier-style case:

> SHEEP IN THE FIELD: Roddy is a farmer. One day he is looking into a field near-by and clearly sees something that looks just like a sheep. Consequently he forms a belief that there is a sheep in the field. Moreover, this belief is true in that there is a sheep in the field in question. However, what Roddy is looking at is not a sheep, but rather a big hairy dog that looks just like a sheep and which is obscuring from view the sheep standing just behind.[6]

In SHEEP IN THE FIELD, Roddy has a justified true belief that *there is a sheep in the field*. But – as this case bears a classic Gettier structure – Roddy doesn't *know* there is a sheep in the field. Why not?

From Greco's perspective, the answer is simple: in SHEEP IN THE FIELD (as well as other Gettier cases), the subject, *S*, believes from an ability and has a true belief, but the fact that *S* believes from an ability is not the most salient part of a causal explanation for why *S* has a true belief – thus no Greco-aptness and a fortiori no knowledge. This is so even though *S*'s believing from ability is *a part* of the total set of causal factors that give rise to their believing truly.

A critic might press back: Why *isn't* cognitive ability the most salient part of the causal explanation for the subject's getting it right in Gettier cases? What are the mechanisms governing explanatory salience that would get this result? According to Greco (2008, 2010) explanatory salience is partially a function of our interests and purposes, and therefore, a function of what is normal or usual in light of these interests and purposes. Given our interests and purposes as information-sharing beings (viz., we as a default want to share and receive good information), our intellectual abilities have a *default salience* in explanations of our true belief. However, as the thought goes, in Gettier cases, this default salience is trumped by something abnormal in the way that the subject acquires a true belief. In effect, Gettier cases involve something akin to a deviant causal chain.[7]

So far, uni-level virtue epistemology's core knowledge thesis is looking good. It not only deals with Gettier cases, but does so in a straightforward way. As far as traditional Gettier cases go, the view gets full marks.

---

[6] This is Pritchard's (2009) variation on a Gettier-style case due originally to Chisholm (1977).
[7] For criticism, see Pritchard (2008).

1.4 Value of Knowledge

One of the trickiest contemporary problems in the theory of knowledge concerns the relationship between the nature of knowledge and the *value* of knowledge. No one denies that knowledge is valuable. But why is it valuable? A knee-jerk answer here holds: because it can get us what we want! Put another way, knowledge is *instrumentally* practically valuable. True, however, we *also* think that knowledge is more valuable than *mere* true belief[8] – viz., true belief that falls short of knowledge. So a sharper question is: *in virtue of what is knowledge more valuable than mere true belief?*

Here is where things quickly complicate. A lesson from Plato's *Meno* is that mere true belief will get us what we want just as well as knowledge. After all, one who truly believes that a given road leads to Larissa is as well served as one who knows that it does.[9]

Explaining why knowledge is more valuable than mere true belief is especially difficult for reliabilist accounts of knowledge, which identify knowledge with reliably produced true belief.[10] This is because reliabilists conceive the difference between knowledge and true belief that falls short of knowledge as a difference in the reliability of the source. But the reliability of a source, as Zagzebski (2003) and Kvanvig (2003) have argued, cannot add value to its product.[11] The value of a good cup of espresso is not increased by the fact that it was made by a reliable espresso machine. (Just consider: a cup of espresso with the same intrinsic qualities, but made by an unreliable machine, would have exactly the same value.) The conclusion, then, seems to be that reliabilism cannot explain why the value of knowledge exceeds that of mere true belief; if (as we think it is) knowledge is more valuable than mere true belief, its value must be explained in some other way.

At this point, a uni-level virtue epistemologist such as Greco has a promising card to play. Remember that part of the virtue epistemologist's 'core triad' of claims includes the *cognitive achievement thesis*:

Cognitive achievement thesis (CAT): Knowledge is a (species of) cognitive achievement.

Cognitive achievement thesis now comes in very handy. If knowledge is always and everywhere an *achievement*, then we can make sense (easily, in fact!) of

---

[8] The core idea needn't implicate that we think knowledge is significantly more valuable than a corresponding mere true belief in the same proposition. For discussion on different ways to capture the driving intuition, see Greco 2010, chapter 6; compare, Hetherington 2018.

[9] Compare, however, Goldberg 2023; Olsson 2007; Williamson 2000.

[10] See, for example, Goldman 1999.   [11] For criticism, see Carter and Jarvis 2012.

why it is better than *mere* true belief. All we need to get that result is to pair CAT with the independently plausible *value of achievements* thesis:

Value of achievements thesis (VOA): All achievements – successes from ability – are finally valuable.

'Final' value is *non-instrumental* value – viz., value something has not just for the sake of something else.[12] The idea captured by VOA – viz., that achievements, as such, have final (non-instrumental) value – is easily motivated by reductio. Consider that if achievements were *merely* instrumentally valuable relative to the target success, then we'd have no reason to prefer, for example, an archery shot that succeeds through skill to one that succeeds just through luck. But we do! And insofar as we do, the best explanation here is that an achievement (a success from ability) is not valuable only insofar as the relevant success is valuable. From CAT, along with VOA, we derive (with no other premises needed) the conclusion that knowledge is finally valuable, and a fortiori, more valuable than *mere* true belief.

At this point, uni-level virtue epistemology is looking great: full-points for *both* the Gettier problem and the value of knowledge problem.

1.5 Temp-Style Cases (Safety without Aptness)

Uni-level virtue epistemology has got some momentum. Let's keep riding it – right up until the point where we see a good reason not to. Recall that one of the uni-level virtue epistemologist's credentials is that it offers an elegant way to rule-out knowledge in Gettier cases. Well, so does another competitor type of view, one that appeals to *safety* rather than aptness to do the trick.

Safety condition (SC): *S*'s belief is safe if and only if in most nearby possible worlds in which *S* continues to form their belief about the target proposition in the same way as in the actual world, the belief continues to be true.[13]

In Gettier cases like SHEEP IN THE FIELD, Roddy's belief is not apt, but it's *also* not safe, with reference to SC. Very easily, Roddy believes falsely in nearby worlds (that there is a sheep in the field) when we hold fixed the way he formed the target belief in the actual world. So, the thesis that knowledge requires safety seems to do just as well as uni-level virtue epistemology does in ruling out Gettier cases as cases of knowledge.

---

[12] See, for example, Rabinowicz and Rønnow-Rasmussen 2000; and, for a classic presentation of this idea, Aristotle in the *Nicomachean Ethics* I.7.
[13] See Pritchard 2005.

Now *this* observation might lead one to reason as follows: if we assume safety is necessary for knowledge,[14] might it also be *sufficient* whenever one's belief is true? And if safe, true belief is *sufficient* for knowledge, then this would make any kind of 'ability' condition whatsoever on knowledge – even a very weak ability condition – at best redundant (if safety entails that a belief derive from ability) and at worst an unnecessarily demanding extra necessary condition.

It's at this point that uni-level virtue epistemology has an important move to make, one that's been developed in different ways by Duncan Pritchard and Ernest Sosa.

The first point to note here is that at least a weak ability condition on knowledge would *not* be made redundant by a safety condition. Some beliefs that are safe are not produced from any ability *whatsoever*. The second and crucial point is that, in cases where safe true belief is not produced from ability, the belief plausibly falls short of knowledge. From these claims it follows that it's *not* the case that safe true belief is sufficient for knowledge. The argument goes as follows:

Safety Insufficiency Argument
1. It's possible that a true belief is both safe and not the product of ability (whatsoever).
2. True beliefs that are safe but not the product of ability (whatsoever) aren't known.
3. If safe true belief is sufficient for knowledge, then it's not the case that beliefs that are safe but not the product of ability (whatsoever) aren't known.
4. Therefore, safe true belief is not sufficient for knowledge.

The interesting premises here are (P1) and (P2). We can support both premises in one fell swoop with Pritchard's case of TEMP:

> TEMP: Temp forms his beliefs about the temperature in the room by consulting a thermometer. His beliefs, so formed, are highly reliable, in that any belief he forms on this basis will always be correct. Moreover, he has no reason for thinking that there is anything amiss with his thermometer. But the thermometer is in fact broken, and is fluctuating randomly within a given range. Unbeknownst to Temp, there is an agent hidden in the room who is in control of the thermostat whose job it is to ensure that every time Temp consults the thermometer the 'reading' on the thermometer corresponds to the temperature in the room. (Pritchard 2012, 260)

---

[14] This is a point we engage with critically in much more detail shortly.

The case of TEMP offers a kind of 'proof of concept' that you can have safety without aptness – and indeed (as per P1), even without the exercise of any ability whatsoever. The helper is doing *all* of the work, as it were, to make sure that Temp's beliefs are true. Moreover, the case of TEMP offers support for (P2). It seems that the disconnect between Temp's own abilities and his getting it right about the temperature in this case suffices to disqualify him as a knower, even though the helper ensures that Temp couldn't easily be wrong when looking at the broken thermometer. It follows, then, that safe, true belief is *not* sufficient for knowledge. So *even if* a safety condition is fit for the purpose of ruling out Gettier cases, knowledge can't simply be a matter of safe, true belief.

What *other* lesson can be gleaned from the case of TEMP? Does it follow that aptness is *necessary* for knowledge? It would be great for the uni-level virtue epistemologist if we *could* draw this conclusion. But we can't; the case of TEMP is a case of safety without aptness, true, but it is *also* a case where not *any* ability is present. All we're entitled to conclude from cases like TEMP is that *some kind of ability condition* on knowledge is necessary. That condition might be weaker than the kind of ability condition that aptness requires.

With this in mind, consider Pritchard's weak ability condition on knowledge:

Weak ability condition on knowledge (WACK): *S* knows that *p* only if *S*'s believing *p* truly is to a significant degree attributable to their cognitive ability.

What does 'to a significant degree attributable' mean? Pritchard is careful to emphasise that the satisfaction of this weak ability condition does *not* imply (though is implied by) Greco's stronger ability condition. Remember that, for Greco, ability must be – in cases of knowledge – *the most salient* part of the total set of causal factors that explains why the subject believes truly.

We'll soon see why Pritchard thinks Greco's ability condition is too strong, and that WACK is better. But for now it should suffice to conclude first that even though safety can rule out Gettier cases just like aptness can, safe true belief isn't sufficient for knowledge. (Thus far, we've seen no reason to think apt belief is *not* sufficient.) Second, cases like TEMP motivate *at least* a weak ability condition such as WACK on propositional knowledge. This is good news for uni-level virtue epistemology; but, equally, it is good news for at least one formidable competitor: Pritchard's (2012) *anti-luck virtue epistemology.*[15]

---

[15] Pritchard's most recent formulation of anti-luck virtue epistemology is *presented as anti-risk virtue epistemology* (2016), which keeps most of the key details the same. Since for our purposes what goes for his anti-luck virtue epistemology will go likewise for the newer version, my presentation of the view will focus on the earlier anti-luck formulation.

1.6 Comparison: Anti-Luck Virtue Epistemology

Keeping score so far: uni-level virtue epistemology of the sort we've been exploring – which identifies knowledge with Greco-aptness – has the following merits; it:

(i)   rules out Gettier cases;
(ii) implies a ready solution to the value problem; and
(iii) rules out knowledge in the TEMP case.

By comparison: although the view that knowledge is safe true belief can (i) rule out Gettier cases just as well as can an identification of knowledge with Greco-aptness, it has no clear explanation for (ii) and outright fails (iii).

Pritchard's (2012) *anti-luck virtue epistemology* is a more difficult competitor.

Anti-luck virtue epistemology (ALVE): *S* knows that *p* iff *S*'s true belief that *p* satisfies both (i) the safety condition (SC); and (ii) WACK.

According to ALVE, SC and WACK are logically independent necessary and jointly sufficient conditions for knowledge. One knows iff one satisfies both SC (which accommodates the insight that knowledge excludes luck) and WACK (which, for Pritchard, is what is motivated theoretically by the intuition we have – for example, as illustrated by cases like TEMP, that knowledge must in some way be the product of ability).

Anti-luck virtue epistemology is tough competition because it (i) rules out Gettier cases (courtesy of the safety condition); and (iii) unlike a simple 'safe true belief' account of knowledge, rules out knowledge in TEMP-style cases, given that WACK is not satisfied in such cases. As for (ii), an explanation for the value of knowledge, the edge still goes to uni-level virtue epistemology, which identifies knowledge with Greco-aptness. *That* view, recall – in conjunction with the VOA thesis – implies that knowledge is finally valuable. However, we can't derive the thesis that knowledge is finally valuable from the conjunction of VOA and WACK. This is because there is a logical gap between WACK and the thesis that knowledge is a (species) of cognitive achievement (CAT).

One might ask whether we're being uncharitable to ALVE here. Perhaps we could interpret WACK in a way that would imply CAT (and thus, in a way that would combine with VOA to generate the result that knowledge is finally valuable)?

What's interesting here is that it is actually important for Pritchard that he does *not* close this gap! Pritchard's ALVE is *designed* in such a way that we *should not* read WACK as implying CAT. But the reason for this insistence – the aim of not ruling out *testimony cases* as cases of knowledge – turns out to be misguided, and so ALVE (unlike Greco-style uni-level virtue epistemologist) sacrifices a solution to the value problem unnecessarily. Let's see just why this is.

1.7 Challenge: Testimony

Here is a case, due to Lackey (2007, 2009), that is often taken to raise trouble for any ability condition on knowledge that is *strong enough* to imply CAT – viz., the view that knowledge always and everywhere involves cognitive achievement.

> CHICAGO VISITOR: Morris wishes to obtain directions to the Sears Tower. He looks around, approaches the first adult passerby that he sees, and asks how to get to his desired destination. The passerby, who happens to be a lifelong resident of Chicago and knows the city extraordinarily well, provides Morris with impeccable directions to the Sears Tower by telling him that it is located two blocks east of the train station. Morris unhesitatingly forms the corresponding true belief. (Lackey 2009, 29).

As Lackey sees it, what explains why Morris got things right has nearly nothing of epistemic interest to do with him and nearly everything of epistemic interest to do with the passerby. Thus, though it is plausible to say that Morris acquired *knowledge* from the passerby,[16] there seems to be no substantive sense in which Morris's getting it right is an achievement of his.

If this is right, then Greco-aptness is too *strong* a requirement for knowledge – it would rule out knowledge in cases like CHICAGO VISITOR. (After all – even though Morris's ability is a *part* of the set of causal factors that give rise to his true belief, it is not *the most salient part* of the set of causal factors.) That is, as Lackey thinks, the epistemic labour of the *testifier*.

It is with reference to CHICAGO VISITOR that we can see why Pritchard thinks ALVE has a key advantage over Greco's view. While ALVE *does* require that a knower satisfy an ability condition, the ability condition Pritchard favours – WACK – is weak enough that it is plausibly *satisfied* in cases like CHICAGO VISITOR. After all, even if Morris's abilities aren't the most salient part of the set of causal factors that explains his success, they are plausibly a *significant* part of the story – and in a way that Temp's abilities are *not* in TEMP.

If this is right, it looks like uni-level virtue epistemology loses its edge over ALVE. As the thought goes, both deal with Gettier cases and the TEMP case,

---

[16] Lackey takes this result to be implied by any (non-sceptical) version of either reductionism or anti-reductionism in the epistemology of testimony.

and uni-level virtue epistemology has the edge in explaining the value of knowledge (given that it includes a commitment to CAT), but *because* of the commitment to CAT, uni-level virtue epistemology problematically excludes knowledge in testimony cases. Perhaps, then, we've got a tie?

I think there are *two* good replies to this on behalf of uni-level virtue epistemologist, which show that the simple knowledge = aptness equivalence needn't – despite initial appearances – actually cede any ground at all to ALVE when it comes to dealing with testimony cases in a satisfactory way, and thus that, at least for all we've considered so far, it retains its edge.

The first strategy of reply continues to unpack uni-level virtue epistemology's knowledge = aptness equivalence along Greco's preferred lines (viz., knowledge = Greco-aptness). The second reply involves swapping out Greco-aptness for Sosa-aptness.

Let's look first at the resources for the champion of 'knowledge = Greco-aptness'. Consider that first, what matters for whether a belief is Greco-apt (and thus, an achievement) is not so much that the testifier is reliable, or that the believer knows that they are, but that the believer themselves *is reliable in the way that they receive and evaluate testimony*. With this observation in mind, Greco thinks, we can appreciate how CHICAGO VISITOR *is underdescribed*.

How is it underdescribed? According to Greco, we can divide Lackey's example into two cases: one where Morris is a reliable receiver of testimony and one where he is not (say, he would ask someone who is visibly confused). Greco thinks that in the first version of the case – where we make explicit that Morris is a reliable receiver of testimony – we should have no trouble both crediting him with knowledge *and* crediting his (ex hypothesi, in this version) reliable abilities as the most salient part of the explanation for why he got it right. In the *second* version of the case, Greco grants that Morris's abilities would not be salient in explaining the success of his belief; but that's also OK, because neither, in the second version of the case, does Morris have knowledge.

Put together, then, Greco's reply to CHICAGO VISITOR-style cases charges his opponent with a bait-and-switch. We are 'baited' (via the trappings of a normal, good testimony case) into thinking that surely Morris has knowledge, and then led to think there is no achievement by drawing attention to the work done by the informant and away from what Morris does. But this dialectical tactic obscures the matter of whether Morris is reliable as a receiver of testimony, which, when he is, should be salient even if the testifier is reliable, and which (when he isn't) will be neither a case of achievement nor knowledge.

1.8 Interlude: Uni-Level Value Epistemology: Greco-Aptness and Sosa-Aptness

If you are convinced by Greco's reply (my students are usually evenly divided!), then uni-level virtue epistemology retains a clear edge over ALVE thus far. If you are not so convinced, then for uni-level virtue epistemology to retain its edge over ALVE (which it retains by dealing with the value problem better than ALVE while *not* ruling out knowledge in testimony cases like CHICAGO VISITOR as ALVE doesn't), it will need to dispense with equating knowledge with Greco-aptness and find a champion other than Greco.

Unfortunately for the friend of the knowledge = Greco-aptness equivalence, there turns out to be a potential problem with Greco's reply. But fortunately for the friend of uni-level virtue epistemology, the problem can be patched by swapping Greco-aptness for Sosa-aptness.

So what is the problem, exactly? Bear with me. Let's grant Greco that CHICAGO VISITOR is underdescribed, and that we can break down the case into two versions – one (V1) where we stipulate Morris is a reliable receiver of testimony, and another (V2) where we stipulate that Morris is not. I think it's fair enough to grant Greco that there is no knowledge in (V2). And this is broadly for reasons similar to why Temp lacks knowledge in TEMP. In (V2) (as in TEMP) not even Pritchard's WACK is satisfied. So the fact that there is no Greco-aptness in (V2) is not a problem for Greco, since it's not a case of knowledge.

The problem for Greco is (V1). Even if we grant that Morris is a reliable receiver of testimony, it is an open question whether these reliable abilities he has would be a particularly *salient* part of a causal explanation for why he got it right, when compared with the abilities of the informant. By Greco's own lights, recall, the mechanisms that govern causal-explanatory salience include our interests and purposes. With reference to our interests and purposes as know-ledge exchangers, he thinks our abilities have a default salience in explaining our beliefs, which can be trumped by abnormal factors. The point worth considering is not that receiving testimony is an abnormal way to get know-ledge – on the contrary – it's that our interests and purposes as knowledge exchangers (which is what governs our causal-explanatory salience attribu-tions) will presumably include the critical fact that we value *reliable sources* of information. But once that point is appreciated, it becomes less clear why – in a given testimonial exchange – our interests and purposes would adjudicate in favour of *our* abilities rather than our *informant's* abilities as being what is most salient in explaining testimonial success. The worry is, then, that by the lights of Greco's own account of what determines causal-explanatory salience, it seems like at best an open question whether in (V1) of the case it should be Morris's or his informant's abilities that are more salient.

Some readers might think Greco has at his disposal some way to 'close' the kind of open-question argument just posed against his diagnosis of (V1)-variations on CHICAGO VISITOR.[17] However, the good news for uni-level virtue epistemology is that the fate of uni-level virtue epistemology doesn't depend on this, as Greco's account of aptness isn't the only game in town.

At this point, it will be helpful to consider *three ways* we might conceive of the connection knowledge requires between a thinker's cognitive ability and their getting it right.

- Option 1: Knowledge requires that cognitive success must be to *a significant degree creditable* to ability (from WACK). This is Pritchard's preference – it has no trouble ruling in knowledge in cases like CHICAGO VISITOR; however, the connection between success and ability captured here (from WACK), recall, does not entail the cognitive achievement thesis (CAT).
- Option 2: Knowledge requires cognitive success for which ability *is the most salient part of the total set of causal factors*[18] for that success (from Greco-aptness). This is Greco's preference – it entails CAT, and so has no trouble at all resolving the value problem; however, the connection between success and ability captured here (from Greco-aptness) is arguably too strong to uncontroversially rule-in cases like CHICAGO VISITOR as cases of know-ledge. It struggles (as we've just seen) even when we limit our focus to V1-style cases.
- Option 3: Knowledge requires success *that manifests ability.*

Option 3 – a new idea to this point – is Sosa's preference. This option is interesting in that it seems to offer the proponent of uni-level virtue epistemol-ogy the tools needed to 'thread the needle' here. That is, Sosa-aptness (which requires that the correctness of a belief manifest ability) plausibly entails CAT *without* succumbing to the kind of problem Greco faced with V1-testimony cases. The possibility of threading this needle becomes apparent when we consider that Greco-aptness (and thus the connection between success and ability captured by Option 2) *suffices* to imply CAT, but it is not *necessary* to imply CAT.

Let's set aside talk of causal-explanatory salience completely now (central to the idea that knowledge = Greco-aptness) and consider the idea, due to Sosa, that achievements are, as described in Option 3, successes that *manifest* ability.

---

[17] For a very different kind of theory, see Greco 2020b. This does however take us beyond the 'Knowledge = Greco-aptness' view (from 2003–10) under consideration here.

[18] See fn. 4.

When do successes manifest ability? They do so when they issue from the exercise of a skill, *not just in any old circumstance*, but when the subject is in proper shape, and properly situated to exercise that skill. What is a skill? A skill is a disposition to succeed when one makes an attempt *while in proper shape and properly situated* to make that kind of attempt.

Even when drugged and in the dark without a basketball, Steph Curry remains skilled at shooting free throws in a way a five-year-old child (also drugged, in the dark, and without a basketball) is not. Steph retains this skill because it remains true of him that *if* he were in proper shape and properly situated, he'd make a free throw reliably enough if he tried. When Steph exercises his free-throw shooting skill *and is in proper shape and properly situated to do so*, then when he makes it, his shot is not *merely* successful, but it also manifests his skill exercised in proper shape and properly situated. To use Sosa's terminology, Steph here manifests his *complete competence* – and in doing so, his success is an achievement, something more valuable (as the kind of attempt it is) than *mere* success which doesn't manifest a complete competence.

Of course, we're talking basketball here and not yet epistemology, but the case of Steph should help us see how 'being most saliently causally explained by ability' is but one way to think about what achievement demands; another way is with reference to the *manifestation* of a complete competence – viz., the manifestation of skill in conditions appropriate for its exercise.

Bringing us back now to epistemology: let's now contrast Greco-aptness with Sosa-aptness.

Sosa-aptness A subject *S*'s belief that *p* is apt iff it is accurate because adroit.[19]

Whereas Greco-aptness unpacks the relevant 'because' in a characterisation of aptness in terms of causal-explanatory salience, Sosa unpacks the 'because' with reference to *competence manifestation*. A belief is accurate because adroit for Sosa iff the accuracy manifests the believer's complete competence.

If the uni-level virtue epistemologist were to identify knowledge with Sosa-aptness rather than with Greco-aptness, there is no problematic 'gap' (as there is with a weak ability condition like WACK) between knowledge and achievement. *Both* Greco-aptness and Sosa-aptness offer independent ways to unpack the core idea – central to achievement – that knowledge is a success because of ability. Crucially, the problem that Greco-aptness faces with Lackey cases doesn't obviously carry over to Sosa-aptness.

---

[19] For this formulation of aptness, see Sosa 2007. It will be modified in later chapters when we distinguish between functional belief and judgement.

Both Greco and Sosa can agree that what matters for knowledge is the reliable abilities of the testimonial recipient. However, we can't attribute Greco-aptness to Morris without inviting questions about causal-explanatory salience that invite us to compare the contribution of the testifier to that of the testimonial receiver. But we can attribute Sosa-aptness to Morris without needing to make any such comparison. After all, to settle whether the 'because' that features in Sosa-aptness is satisfied (accurate because adroit), we ask just whether Morris's believing correctly manifested his complete competence.

Suppose we, following Greco, divide CHICAGO VISITOR into two versions (V1 and V2). From the idea that knowledge = Sosa-aptness, we get the result that Morris lacks both aptness and knowledge in V2 (the same result Greco got), but – in V1 – we get the result that Morris's belief is apt, and he knows. And we get this result *without* needing to prove any comparative claim about whether Morris did more than the testifier did – a comparison that we've seen looks like a trap. What matters is *just* whether Morris's success manifested a complete competence – something it can manifest in a way that could suffice for achievement *even if* at the end of the day the testifier's abilities are comparatively more salient in explaining Morris's success.

At this point, then – for those keeping score – uni-level virtue epistemology continues to retain its lead over the competition, *at least* so long as we unpack aptness as Sosa-aptness rather than Greco-aptness.

The situation complicates a bit further for uni-level virtue epistemology when we move to the testing ground of fake barns.

1.9 Challenge: Fake Barns

Without further suspense – consider *FAKE BARN*:

> *FAKE BARN*: Using his reliable perceptual faculties, Barney forms a true belief that the object in front of him is a barn. Barney is indeed looking at a barn. Unbeknownst to Barney, however, most objects that look like barns in these parts are in fact barn façades.

Does Barney *know* he is looking at a barn? This is controversial. On the one hand, a series of recent empirical studies suggests that most people attributed knowledge in barn façade cases. Experiments by Colaço and colleagues (2014), Turri and colleagues (2015), and Turri (2016) reported that participants were more inclined than not to attribute knowledge in fake barn cases (with a majority of 80 per cent of participants registering this view in Turri's (2016) study.[20] Some epistemologists, including Hetherington (1998, 2013), Baumann (2014), and

---

[20] For discussion, see Carter et al. 2018, section 3, 2016, section 3.3.

Sosa (more on this soon!) are also inclined to attribute knowledge in cases like FAKE BARN.

However, it's fair to say that the tide in mainstream epistemology is with the *opposition* here. The reason is simple. FAKE BARN shares a common feature with traditional Gettier cases, which is that the target belief is *unsafe*, with reference to the core canonical idea of what safety requires. Recall the safety condition (SC) holds that S's belief is safe if and only if in most nearby possible worlds in which S continues to form their belief about the target proposition in the same way as in the actual world, the belief continues to be true.

Standard Gettier cases (e.g., SHEEP IN THE FIELD) feature unsafe beliefs with reference to SC, but crucially, so do FAKE BARN cases. After all, Barney continues to believe 'there is a barn' in very close worlds where his glance happens to fall upon one of the many fakes. If satisfying SC is necessary for knowledge, then FAKE BARN-style cases support a simple template argument against uni-level virtue epistemology, and it's an argument that Greco and Sosa respond to very differently.

Here's the template argument.[21]

Fake barn argument against a knowledge-aptness equivalence
1. Uni-level virtue epistemology holds that knowledge is apt belief.
2. If a theory of knowledge holds that knowledge is apt belief, then it allows unsafe beliefs to count as knowledge.
3. If a theory of knowledge allows unsafe beliefs to count as knowledge, then that view is incorrect.
4. Therefore uni-level virtue epistemology is incorrect.

A few preliminary points. First, Pritchard's ALVE is not a target of this argument for *two* reasons: (i) ALVE, despite having an ability condition (WACK), does not hold that knowledge is apt belief; and (ii) by virtue of embracing SC as a necessary condition on knowledge, ALVE doesn't allow unsafe beliefs to count as knowledge. Second, note that those who would identify knowledge with Greco-aptness or Sosa-aptness are direct targets of the argument. And FAKE BARN offers strong support for Premise 2, given that Barney's belief in FAKE BARN seems (at least prima facie) to be *both* apt and unsafe.

Here are the most obvious available strategies in resopnse to the Fake Barn Argument for one who would embrace the view that knowledge is apt belief:

- *Strategy 1*: deny that knowledge requires satisfying the safety condition (SC) (and so deny P3 in the Fake Barn Argument)

---

[21] See, for example, Pritchard 2012; Kallestrup and Pritchard 2012; and Lackey 2009.

- *Strategy 2*: deny that the subject in FAKE BARN has an apt belief (and so deny P2 in the Fake Barn Argument)
- *Strategy 3*: deny that the subject in FAKE BARN fails to satisfy SC (and so deny P2 in the Fake Barn Argument).

Greco takes Strategy 2. He accordingly denies what Pritchard and Sosa are in agreement about – which is that cases like FAKE BARN feature apt belief that fail the SC – and Greco does this by denying that Barney has an apt belief in these cases.

Remember that, when we introduced Greco-aptness, we unpacked *two* substantive components of his view – one to do with causal-explanatory salience, and the other with the nature of cognitive abilities, which Greco understands as *environment-relative* stable dispositions to believe truly reliably. The environment-relativity clause turns out to be important to his taking Strategy 2 in response to the Fake Barn Argument. According to Greco (2010, chapter 5), even though – relative to normal environments – we may assume that Barney can discriminate between barns and non-barns, relative to the kind of environment he's in in FAKE BARN, he does not have such an ability.

This way of responding to the argument, however, comes with some pretty serious costs in order to avoid allowing aptness to persist along with lack of safety construed as SC. Not only is the cost serious, but as we'll see shortly, it's not necessary to pay it.

There are two arguments against taking Strategy 2, an argument from linguistic attribution data, and an overgeneralisation argument. The former, a version of which is put forward by Pritchard, draws attention to how our patterns of ability attribution don't line up with Greco's inclination to deny that Barney possesses and exercises in FAKE BARN the cognitive ability that we would attribute to him in normal environments with no fakes around. The crux of Pritchard's point is that – at least going by the way we ordinarily attribute ability – we are inclined to say it's the *same* ability (e.g., say, to play the piano) that one possesses and exercises, *even in* circumstances where one has to take more things into account than normal as it is when one needn't do so. We don't distinguish between an ability-to-play-the-piano-indoors (say, in a crowded room of people talking) from an ability-to-play-the-piano-outdoors with no one around. We describe this as the *same* ability to play the piano that one exercises in both situations. Taking this linguistic point a step further – compare a pianist who, in Scenario 1, plays a piano (say, the song 'Für Elise') in a normal recital hall, and in Scenario 2, the same pianist plays 'Für Elise' in a different recital hall which *very easily* could have been flooded with water, but which luckily was not. It is certainly intuitive to say that this pianist possesses and exercises the very same ability (e.g., to play 'Für Elise' on the piano) in both scenarios. And what goes for the pianist with 'Für Elise' goes, *mutatis mutandis* for two versions of the FAKE BARN case we might imagine – viz., Version 1 with no fakes around (a normal case) and Version 2, with fakes around. Just as it seems intuitive to say the same ability is possessed and exercised in Version 1 of the 'Für Elise' case as in Version 2, likewise, it would be felicitous to say that Barney possesses and exercises the same ability in Version 1 (a good case) as in the FAKE BARN case. In short, then, the linguistic argument recognises as felicitous of a kind of ability attribution pattern (in good environment/bad environment pairs), and in a way that suggests denying Barney an ability to spot barns in fake barn country, when we'd attribute it to him otherwise, at least goes against ability attribution patterns.

The reader might not put much stock in the evidential weight of linguistic attribution patterns. After all, patterns of use offer at best indirect and defeasible evidence about the nature of the phenomena referred to.

But even if one were to satisfactorily press back against the above linguistic argument, an *overgeneralisation argument* lies waiting in the wings. Consider now the case of Simone, due to Sosa (2010a):

> SIMONE: Simone is a skilled pilot in training who could easily be, not in a real cockpit, but in a simulation, with no tell-tale signs. Trainees are strapped down asleep in their cockpits, and only then awakened. Let us suppose Simone to be in a real cockpit, flying a real plane, and shooting targets accurately.

How should we evaluate Simone's shots in this case? They are accurate *ex hypothesi*. However, it seems they are not merely accurate. It is not as though we are assuming Simone is a complete beginner who just happens to be hitting the targets by luck. She is a skilled pilot, and (unlike, say, archery shots that are fired randomly) Simone's shots seem in an important sense to be ability-implicating achievements, shots that succeed because of the ability she has.[22]

This very plausible reading of SIMONE however provides the basis for an overgeneralization argument against Greco's commitment to environment-relative ability attributions. The argument runs as follows:

Overgeneralisation argument against environment-relative ability attributions
1. Assumption (for reductio): Barney doesn't have the ability to spot (genuine) barns in FAKE BARN because his doing so is *unsafe* (with reference to SC) – he fails in close near-by worlds where he continues to believe he is looking at a barn.

---

[22] See also Carter 2021a, 3496–7.

2. Simone's shots at (genuine) targets are unsafe (with reference to SC) in SIMONE – she fails in close near-by worlds where she continues to shoot but hits only simulated targets.
3. If Barney doesn't have the ability to spot barns in FAKE BARN, then Simone doesn't have the ability to hit real targets in SIMONE.
4. If Simone's shots at real targets are achievements, then Simone exercises (and therefore possesses) an ability to hit real targets.
5. Simone's shots at real targets are achievements.
6. Simone exercises (and therefore possesses) an ability to hit real targets in SIMONE.
7. Therefore, the assumption in (1) is false.

In the face of this overgeneralization argument, it looks like Greco's options are limited: either (i) deny Simone the ability that seems to be implicated by her achievement in SIMONE; *or* (ii) reject the parity premise (3) by disputing the structural parity between FAKE BARN and SIMONE.[23]

Suppose one – not optimistic about the first strategy – were to attempt the latter route and quibble about the parity premise (3). For instance, one might point out that the details of the case aren't *exactly* analogous; after all, as one line of thought might go, Simone seems to wake up in a good environment, which is what she finds herself in. Her case is, as it were, structurally analogous not to FAKE BARN but to a version of the fake barn case where Barney *easily* could have turned down the road that leads to fake barn country but just so happened to choose a different road – and so forms beliefs that are safe.

The above rationale for rejecting the parity premise (3) raises an interesting question about how to think about our application of SC – we'll circle back to this with a critical eye very shortly. However, more pressingly for now, rejecting such a parity principle is not going to work because exact analogues of the fake barn case can be constructed where the intuition that an ability-implicating achievement is present is just as strong as in SIMONE, but where there is no room at all to quibble about any issues to do with structural parity. Consider now Pritchard's case FORCEFIELD:

> FORCEFIELD: Archie is an archer who arbitrarily selects his target and skilfully fires his arrow, hitting the target. Unbeknownst to Archie, all the other potential targets in the field are surrounded by invisible forcefields that

---

[23] For critical discussion here, see Sosa 2021. Note that Sosa (2021), by reference to the theory of default assumptions, now treats FAKE BARN and SIMONE differently, as possessing not only animal, but also reflective knowledge. This new move marks a departure from the standard version of his view, which denies reflective knowledge to both. The new view, which I lack space to fully engage with here, introduces the concept of secure knowledge full well, where one's competences are securely in place. See Sosa 2021, 186.

would have repelled his arrow, and as a co sequence, Archie would not have hit the target had he fired his arrow at any of them. Fortunately, Archie happened to have chosen the target that is force field-free.

Archie is really just like Barney – the only difference is that Barney is firing intellectual shots (beliefs) targeted at barns, and Archie is firing literal shots (arrows) at targets. Since all parties agree Barney's beliefs fail the SC, we should also accept Archie's shots are analogously unsafe. And yet, as the point goes, it's hard to deny (at least as much as it is in SIMONE) that the case features an ability-implicating achievement.

So where does this all leave us? Consider that we've already seen that uni-level virtue epistemology, construed as the view that knowledge = Greco-aptness struggled with testimony cases in a way that the view that knowledge = Sosa-aptness does not. And now it looks like the view also seems to struggle with fake barn cases. Greco's strategy in response to the *Fake Barn Argument* was to deny (as we've just seen, problematically) that Barney has the relevant ability in FAKE BARN, and thus, to deny that FAKE BARN is a case that features both aptness *and* unsafety. But *this* opens Greco up to the overgeneralisation reductio.

Question: Can the identification of knowledge with Sosa-aptness do better? This is a difficult question, but ultimately, the answer will be a qualified 'yes'.

A first point to note, in unpacking how a proponent of the knowledge = Sosa-aptness equivalence will respond to the Fake Barn Argument, is that a proponent of Sosa-aptness does not, *and should not*, deny the basic idea that abilities are dispositions we articulate with reference to *environments* (broadly speaking) that are suitable to their manifestation. Remember, we've *already seen* that Sosa characterises a skill (alternatively: 'inner-most competence') to do something, ϕ, as a disposition to succeed reliably enough when one makes a ϕ attempt *when in proper shape and properly situated*. On this way of thinking, it doesn't count against an archer's possessing an archery skill, for instance, if the archer would almost always miss *when shooting in high winds in the dark*. To test for archery skill, we ask whether the archer would succeed reliably enough in circum-stances that include the archer's (i) being in a shape that is suitable to archery (awake, alert) and a *situation* that is suitable to archery (e.g., normal winds, enough light, oxygen, etc.).

But isn't *that* already relativising ability/skill to environments, and if so, won't Sosa be required to deny, *just like Greco explicitly does*, that Barney possesses and exercises the relevant skill when he is in barn façade country?

It's worth being very careful here, because even though Sosa *does* relativise skill to environments construed broadly as set out here, he does not deny (and is not committed to denying) that Barney possesses and exercises skill (indeed, a complete competence!) in fake barn country, and even when his belief is unsafe by the lights of SC. The reason here is that – as Sosa sees it – when Barney is positioned towards a real barn he *is* properly situated to exercise the skill he has – a disposition to spot barns when in proper shape and when in the presence of a barn (i.e., which is the proper situation for exercising that competence). Barney continues to have a complete competence in fake barn country, so long as what he's looking at is a real barn.

Against this background, we can now appreciate how a uni-level virtue epistemologist who identifies knowledge with Sosa-aptness can respond to the Fake Barn Argument. The strategy will be to affirm Barney's belief as apt, rather than to (*a la* Greco) deny that it is apt. And by regarding Barney's belief as apt, the proponent of knowledge = Sosa-aptness is thereby attributing to Barney both apt belief and *knowledge*.

Since Barney's belief is obviously unsafe by the lights of (SC), this then leaves the proponent of knowledge = Sosa-aptness taking Strategy 1 rather than Strategy 2.

- **Strategy 1: deny that knowledge requires satisfying the SC (and so deny P3 in the Fake Barn Argument)**.
- ~~Strategy 2: deny that the subject in FAKE BARN has an apt belief (and so deny P2 in the Fake Barn Argument).~~
- Strategy 3: deny that the subject in FAKE BARN fails to satisfy SC (and so deny P2 in the Fake Barn Argument).

Let's look at some ex ante benefits of going this route. It allows a proponent of knowledge = Sosa-aptness to enjoy all the benefits of uni-level virtue epistemology that have been racked up so far (Gettier problem, value of knowledge, TEMP cases, testimony cases) – and to escape the Fake Barn Argument while sidestepping the overgeneralisation argument and associated argument from linguistic data that face Greco's Strategy 2.

The price to be paid, of course, is rejecting the safety condition – *as formulated above* (viz., as SC) – as necessary for knowledge. Let's now look more squarely at this option, consider why it's rarely taken, and whether the proponent of knowledge = Sosa-aptness might be able to jettison SC gracefully – by maintaining something close enough.

1.10 Sosa-Aptness and Safety

The platitude that knowledge in some way 'excludes luck' is more or less sacrosanct.[24] What's been centrally contested by epistemologists is not whether

---

[24] See, for example, Pritchard 2007, 2015. Compare Hetherington 2013.

an anti-luck platitude is sacrosanct but rather how we should specify the specific sense in which knowledge should be thought to exclude luck.

The two most notable attempts to make progress here are due to Nozick (1981) and then Pritchard (e.g., 2005).[25] Nozick thought the sense in which knowledge excludes luck is captured by the thesis that knowledge excludes *insensitive* beliefs – viz., beliefs a thinker would continue to hold even if they were false.[26] Pritchard popularised the idea that the sense in which knowledge excludes luck is better captured by the thesis that knowledge excludes *unsafe* belief – beliefs a thinker *could easily have been wrong about* given how they were formed. The standard (although not the only) modal characterisation of safety is given by SC.

One huge mark *for* Pritchard over Nozick is that – even though *both* conditions are good enough to rule out knowledge in both standard Gettier cases as well as in FAKE BARN – sensitivity is really *too strong*. I won't rehearse the various objections to the strength of sensitivity here,[27] other than to draw attention to one comparative point about the strength of sensitivity versus SC, which nicely illustrates a reason to prefer SC.

Pick any sceptical hypothesis you might like – say, the hypothesis that you are a brain in a vat fooled by misleading sensory evidence into believing you're not a brain in a vat. The sceptic gains a footing on us dialectically if we *never* know the denials of such hypotheses. But that is what would follow from the view that knowledge requires sensitive belief; you'd keep thinking you were *not* a brain in a vat being fooled by misleading sensory evidence *even if you were*.

By comparison, SC implies no such result, so long as the BIV scenario is not *in fact* a close possibility. So long as the BIV scenario obtains only in far-off worlds, it can still be the case that, when you believe (in the actual world) that the BIV scenario doesn't obtain, you couldn't *easily* have been wrong about this; there are, on this supposition, no *nearby* worlds where the scenario holds. This is so *even if* we concede that there are far off worlds where you're wrong. For safety, the far-off worlds don't matter. For sensitivity, they do.

This and other objections to sensitivity as a necessary condition on knowledge (including the worry that accepting it requires denying the closure principle – though we can set this aside) make Pritchard's 'safety-based' modal condition look like an attractive 'anti-luck' codicil on knowledge. It seems to get the benefits of sensitivity (when it comes to ruling out knowledge in Gettier cases and fake barn cases) but without the baggage.

---

[25] Though for a notable precursor to Pritchard's (2005), see Sosa 1999.
[26] For an overview, see Mechior 2019, chapter 2.
[27] For some notable lines of argument, see Pritchard 2012; and Sosa 2007, chapter 2.

Let's assume then that the SC does better than sensitivity as an anti-luck condition on knowledge. Does that mean we should accept SC as it stands? Pritchard (2012) takes it that the thesis that knowledge requires safe belief is really a *platitude* about knowledge – such that we're simply not talking about knowledge anymore if we're talking about beliefs that could 'easily have been false'. If right this would be a platitude that misaligns with folk attributions in fake barn cases, but let's set this aside and grant for now that Pritchard does seem to be on to something here, in thinking that beliefs that could (under some description) *easily be false* fall short of knowledge.

Even on this concession, though, let's remember that Pritchard himself doesn't think that the sacrosanct platitude about knowledge under the description of safety is that knowledge requires one's belief couldn't easily have been false *simpliciter*. Such a flat-footed formulation, which doesn't overtly relativise safety to *the way the subject formed the belief in the actual world* would be subject to easy counterexamples. (For example, you surely know you're in pain when it's *excruciating pain*. This is so even if you might *very easily* have believed you were in pain in the presence of a discomfort that is not really pain.)[28]

What is needed to make an SC (which ossifies the idea that knowledge requires you couldn't easily have been wrong) precise enough to be plausible is that the formulation be *overtly relational* so as to index the target belief to at least *some aspects of the belief formation in the actual world*, which would ensure that we 'skip over' near-by worlds where – using the above case as an example – you believe you have a headache but only do so with mild discomfort.

A popular way to make safety overtly relational in this way is to *reject* that knowledge must be safe (simpliciter) in favour of the more overtly relational statement that knowledge must be *basis-relative* safe:

Basis-relative safety condition (BRSC) A belief *p* is basis-relative safe just in case: In close worlds where *S* believes *p* on basis *B*, *p* is true.

This is tantamount to the plausible idea that knowledge requires that one couldn't easily be wrong *holding fixed the basis on which one in fact forms their belief* in the actual world.

That said, notice that Pritchard's formulation of SC is overtly relational just as this 'basis relative safety' formulation BRSC is – only it overtly relativises safety to a more neutrally described parameter than a 'basis' – viz., to the relevant 'way' one forms their belief about the target proposition in the actual world. Recall:

---

[28] This example is due to Sosa (2007, chapter 2).

Safety condition (SC): S's belief is safe if and only if in most nearby possible worlds in which S continues to form their belief about the target proposition *in the same way as in the actual world*, the belief continues to be true.

A point that now bears emphasis is that Pritchard has hardly 'rejected safety' *simply by rejecting safety simpliciter in favour of an overtly relational formulation of safety*. But once this point is appreciated, it would seem quite odd to suppose that *embracing* the core safety insight (i.e., that knowing requires you couldn't easily have been wrong) but simply opting for a different way (than SC) to characterise the respect in which it is overtly relational should automatically incur one with the theoretical cost of 'rejecting safety'.

Interestingly, that is *just what the proponent of Sosa-aptness does:* like Pritchard, a proponent of the view that knowledge is equivalent to Sosa-aptness both:

(i) accepts (like Pritchard) the core idea at the heart of safety as a condition on knowledge – viz., the idea that knowers couldn't easily have been incorrect; and

(ii) rejects (also, like Pritchard) a *non-overtly relational* characterisation of safety aimed at capturing the insight in (i).

The rejection of SC by the proponent of Sosa-aptness is *merely* a rejection of the *specific characterisation of the respect in which safety is overtly relational* that is captured in SC, and it is against a background of agreement with proponents of SC about (i) and (ii).

What the friend of Sosa-aptness positively holds is that the *right* overtly relational characterisation of safety should be with reference to near-by worlds where we hold fixed not the basis (as per BRSC) or the way the belief was formed (SC), but rather, something else – namely, the seat/shape/situation tuple that corresponds with the exercise of a complete competence.

Take, for example, an ordinary perceiver in good conditions, looking at a red wall (no tricks!). On the assumption that knowledge is type-identical to Sosa-apt belief, it follows that for our perceiver to know the wall is red, their true belief that it is red must issue from the exercise of a *complete competence*. This would implicate that our perceiver possess and exercise a disposition to perceive red walls reliably *when in* proper shape and properly situated to do so, and they *are* in proper shape and properly situated. We can 'extract' an overtly relational safety condition from the above characterisation of Sosa-aptness. After all, *if* our perceiver correctly judges that the wall is red, but we add to the story that they *would easily be wrong* when exercising their disposition to judge red walls when in good shape (sober, alert) and in situations appropriate to exercising visual-perceptual faculties, then their belief in the actual world will *thereby* not manifest their complete competence.

In sum, the complete competence manifestation requirement on knowledge *ensures* that knowledgeable beliefs must be what we can call 'SSS-relative safe': such beliefs must be such that are not false in close worlds where we hold fixed the relevant seat/shape/situation conditions that correspond. This idea is captured in the following principle:

Correctness attribution principle: For any correct belief . . . that *p*, its correctness is attributable to a competence only if it derives from the exercise of that competence in conditions appropriate for its exercise, *where that exercise in those conditions would not too easily have issued a false belief . . .*) (my italics).

Thus, we can add SSS-relative safety (which is implied by the Correctness Attribution Principle) to our growing list of overtly relational characterisations of safety, which include both BSRC and SC.

SSS-relative Safety: A belief is SSS-relative safe just in case: In close worlds where *S* believes *p* from skill *S* exercised in the actual world along with the shape *Sh* and Situation *Si* that correspond with skill *S*, *p* is true.[29]

SSS-relative safety effectively ensures that knowers couldn't easily be wrong *in the conditions that matter* for the exercise of the complete competence implicated by aptness and thus by knowing.

Zooming back out now – we can appreciate with more clarity how the proponent of knowledge = Sosa-aptness pursues Strategy 1 in resisting the Fake Barn Argument. The full diagnosis of FAKE BARN is as follows: Barney's belief *is* apt because, Barney's belief issues from a complete barn-spotting competence. He exercises his barn-spotting skill *while in proper shape and while properly situated to do so*. On the point about being properly situated: this is ensured by the fact that he is situated with respect to a real barn. In that situation, not easily would he have (while in proper shape) confused the barn with something else. His belief in FAKE BARN can be appreciated as apt and by extension SSS-safe, even if not SC-safe.

This fuller unpacking of Strategy 1 reveals an important lesson. To say that a friend of knowledge = Sosa-aptness preserves aptness in FAKE BARN *only by giving up safety* is misleading. It is more accurate to say that what is given up is just the particular way of overtly relativising safety that is captured by SC – and against a background of appreciating that *all* contemporary exponents of a

---

[29] This is modified version of a formulation captured by Greco (2020, 5152).

safety condition on knowledge reject the thesis that knowledge requires safe belief that couldn't easily have been wrong *simpliciter*.

The real question that arises now isn't 'how bad is the cost to giving up safety?' but, rather, whether there is any good reason to prefer SC-safety (or some other basis-relative safety condition, such as BSRC) to SSS-safety. *Both* SC and SSS-safety, we've seen, accommodate the core insight that knowledge 'excludes luck'. For views that incorporate SC, knowledge excludes luck in the way that beliefs that couldn't easily have been false given the way they were formed in the actual world exclude luck. For views that incorporate SSS-safety, knowledge excludes luck in the way that success from competence in general excludes luck.

1.11 Dreaming and (SSS- and SC-) Safety

I want to suggest now that not only does a proponent of SSS-safety not 'give up' safety in any interesting sense (which we've already seen to be the case), but the proponent of SSS-safety also has an important *anti-sceptical advantage* over the proponent of SC-safety.

Remember how the proponent of SC-safety claimed an anti-sceptical advantage over the proponent of sensitivity by pointing to *remote* (i.e., BIV-style) sceptical scenarios, our beliefs about the non-obtaining of which remain SC-safe even though insensitive? The proponent of SSS-safety proposes to co-opt this style of argument on those who hold knowledge requires SC-safe belief by pointing, instead, to *non-remote* sceptical scenarios – and in particular, the *dreaming hypothesis*.

Take, for example, Descartes' belief that he is looking at a fire. Now add, not implausibly, to the story, that very easily, Descartes could be dreaming this, as he might be when tired and resting his eyes.[30] It doesn't take any kind of radical departure from how things are in the actual world for the scenario to obtain where Descartes is simply dreaming and forming false beliefs about what is around him. All that has to happen – a relatively *easy* possibility – is for him to nod off. For a fuller development of this point, see Carter and Cowan (2023).

Acknowledgement of this point about the modal nearness of the obtaining of the dream possibility, however, reveals a problem for SC-safety that is *inapplicable* to SSS-safety, such that the former comparatively struggles to vindicate basic perceptual knowledge in the good case when we are awake.

---

[30] While these descriptive assumptions simplify the example, the point here needn't rely on them. Ordinarily enough, we fall asleep as part of the course of the normal functioning of our faculties; in this respect, sleeping and dreaming are a mundane part of the actual world rather than a radical departure from it.

The argument has two parts: the first part of the argument holds that if it is conceded that, for a given perceptual belief that we form, it is true that we easily could be dreaming, then (i) SC-safety fails. The rationale is that perceptual beliefs are *SC-unsafe* through the nearness of the dream possibility given that, in near-by worlds where one is dreaming, one hosts false beliefs in the relevantly same way (or on the relevantly same kind of sensory basis.)[31]

The second part of the argument emphasises *why* our ordinary perceptual beliefs can remain both apt and SSS-safe *despite* being unsafe with reference to SC-safety. The key theoretical point here is that – as we've seen in cases like SIMONE, FAKE BARN, and so on – cases of aptness (and thus SSS-safety) can feature unsafe (by the lights of SC-safety) belief. And our perceptual beliefs, as the thought goes, are just another instance of that: aptness without SC-safety. As Sosa maintains, 'What dreams render vulnerable is only this: either the perceptual competence of the believer or the appropriate normalcy of the conditions for its exercise.' However, as long as those conditions do *in fact* hold when one is awake, then the correctness of one's belief can derive from them.

Here it will be helpful to draw attention again to the correctness attribution principle, which effectively 'links' aptness with SSS-safety. According to that principle, for any correct belief that *p*, its correctness is attributable to a (complete) competence (such that the belief is then apt) when it derives from the exercise of that competence in conditions appropriate for its exercise, *where that exercise in those conditions would not too easily have issued a false belief.* When Descartes is *in fact awake* (and thus in good shape) and perceiving what is around him in epistemically friendly conditions, his beliefs can accordingly derive from his complete competence, and as such be SSS-safe, *even if* Descartes could very easily have been in the *wrong* shape or situation! The nearness of the dream scenario renders the obtaining of the shape and situation conditions *fragile* – as the thought goes, big deal! So long as they *do* obtain, the perceiver is in the market for aptness.

Thus: whereas FAKE BARN is a case of aptness and SSS-safety without SC-safety where the *situation* relevant for exercising the relevant competence is rendered fragile, in ordinary perception cases, we likewise have aptness and SSS-safety without SC-safety, but where it is the *shape* rather than the situation that is rendered fragile.

The champion of SC safety will attempt to resist the first part of the argument, and so will deny that our ordinary perceptual beliefs are *not* SC-safe. However, as we'll see, the strategies for pressing back all face their own problems – which

---

[31] For a helpful statement of this line of argument, see Sosa 2007, chapter 2. See also the final pages of Sosa 2010a.

is why, ultimately, the proponent of SSS-safety does maintain an advantage here.

One strategy is to insist that even if the *nearness* of the obtaining of the dreaming hypothesis is not disputed, we should reject that its nearness matters (for SC safety) on the basis that we are not actually forming *beliefs* in dreams, but merely *imagining* we are. Think of it this way: a belief is unsafe, by the lights of SC-safety, only if, given how you form the target belief in the actual world, your belief is false in near-by worlds. If, when dreaming, you are imagining and never forming any beliefs at all, then we know *a priori* that you aren't forming any false beliefs at all when dreaming. Thus, the modal proximity of the dreaming hypothesis is orthogonal to the safety of the target belief.

This is a very interesting strategy.[32] But it's not one that a proponent of SC-safety will want to stake the farm on. First, relying on this strategy requires the proponent of SC-safety to embrace an *unorthodox* account of dreaming, one that radically departs from the idea – widespread since the *Meditations* – that dreaming is a genuine sceptical scenario. Moreover, although Sosa and other virtue epistemologists are impressed by the imagination model of dreaming, Sosa concedes, rightly I think, that it would be a mistake for the *virtue epistemologist* to stake their response to dream scepticism on a strategy that relies inescapably on a rejection of the orthodox conception of dreaming. Likewise, and by parity of reasoning, it is better dialectically for the proponent of SC-safety to be able to vindicate ordinary perceptual knowledge in the face of the nearness of the dream scenario in a way that is compatible with the orthodox conception of dreaming on which we can form beliefs while dreaming.

A second available strategy for the proponent of SC-safety will be to contest instead whether the obtaining of the dream hypothesis is really modally close, at least, in everyday cases of our perceptual beliefs. Such a strategy commits one to maintaining that not only is the BIV-scenario not something that happens in near-by worlds, but *neither* is the dreaming scenario. Given the frequency of dreaming in the actual world, and how little has to happen for one to fall asleep and dream, the burden would then be on the proponent of SC-safety to defend (contrary to common-sense thinking about dreams) that the scenario is not modally close in a way that would bear on the safety of ordinary perceptual beliefs. As with the first strategy, this is not a desirable move for the friend of SC-safety – as it again concedes SC-safety to be a condition on knowledge only

---

[32] For discussion, see Sosa 2007, chapter 2; and Ichikawa 2009.

for those (anti-sceptical!) epistemologists willing to embrace other substantively contentious theses.

A third strategy is comparatively more promising for the friend of SC-safety, and that is to deny that there is any way that we form beliefs when we dream that is relevantly the same as the way we form (e.g., perceptually based) beliefs when awake.[33] From *this* denial, we then get the result that even if we accept (*contra* the first strategy) the orthodox conception of dreams (viz., that we form *bona fide* beliefs in dreams), *and* accept further (*contra* the second strategy) that dreaming scenarios are modally close, it remains *false* that our perceptual beliefs when awake are unsafe. It is false because on this third strategy it's not the case that *holding fixed the relevant way we formed the target belief in the actual world* – a way that excludes the way we form beliefs when dreaming – there are close worlds where we believe falsely in dreams.

This third strategy looks, on the face of things, more promising than the first two. There are, however, two weaknesses. First, note that the formulation of SC, as it stands, seems ambiguous as to whether 'the relevant way' the belief was formed in the actual world is broad enough (or not) to accommodate the sceptic's presumption that we form beliefs the same way in the good case as we do in a case where a sceptical scenario obtains. If not, why not?

Second, let's think a bit about the dialectical strategy of *relying* (indeed, however it is ultimately argued for) on there *not* being (as the sceptic supposes) any way of belief forming such that we form a belief in this way in the good case as well as when a sceptical scenario obtains. Such a strategy effectively relies on *external bases* in order to respond to dream scepticism. Appealing to external bases (thus, denying a common basis on which one believes in the good and bad case) commits one further to holding that we can *also* set aside threat of BIV-style scepticism on the grounds that the BIV lacks some basis that sustains our beliefs in the good case.[34]

More generally: this strategy simply takes for granted the falsity of the sceptic's assumption which we'd need to grant to the sceptic in order to even make sense of the idea that there is a shared basis or way one forms a belief in the good case and the bad case, such that one would (in the bad case) be forming beliefs *falsely* in that (relevantly) same way.

An advantage for the virtue epistemologist (who relies on SSS-safety, not SC-safety) is becoming clearer. The very idea that knowledge = apt belief is

---

[33] If we think of SC-safety as capturing a (generic) kind of basis-relative safety, then, we can think of this third strategy as denying that there is any basis common to the good case and the bad case.

[34] For discussion on this point, see Sosa 2007, 27; compare Lasonen-Aarnio 2023.

a thoroughly *externalist* thesis – just as is any view that incorporates SC-safety as a necessary condition on knowledge. Crucially, within the camp of externalist responses to scepticism, the more powerful externalist anti-sceptical strategies will be at least capable of *granting* the sceptic whatever internalist-friendly assumptions they need in order to formulate the genuine sceptical hypotheses they take to be epistemologically vexing. By depending on external bases (by which they could claim one doesn't form beliefs in the relevantly same way when dreaming) the proponent of SC-safety isn't in a position to grant the sceptic much at all. The virtue epistemologist for whom knowledge is apt belief, belief that is at most SSS-safe but not SC safe, is here in the stronger position. While a *form* of externalism, it is able to grant the sceptic a key premise, one that is plausibly intuitive enough to have led dreaming scepticism to need a response in the first place.

Taking this all together, it looks like the friend of SSS-safety can (with reference to dream scepticism), claim an anti-sceptical advantage over SC-safety much as the proponent of SC-safety claimed an anti-sceptical advantage over the proponent of sensitivity.

1.12 Scoreboard So Far

The road so far looks like good news for the proponent of uni-level virtue epistemology who identifies knowledge with Sosa-aptness.

We've seen that this view more than holds its own against the competition across the six test main metrics we've reviewed: (i) the Gettier problem; (ii) the Value of Knowledge; (ii) TEMP-cases; (iv) CHICAGO VISITOR; (v) FAKE BARN; (vi) dreaming-based scepticism.

To help the reader keep track visually, I've rated each of the four views with one of three rough ratings along each of these metrics, based on what we've uncovered in this section:

✓ = strong response
? = dubious or unclear response
x = weak response

The result seems to be that knowledge = Sosa-aptness is in the lead, followed by knowledge = Greco-aptness and ALVE occupying a second tier, followed by the view that knowledge is safe, true belief.[35]

---

[35] Note that we've not considered the possible view, weaker than ALVE, on which knowledge is true belief + WACK. Such a view gets the wrong result in standard Gettier cases (which feature true beliefs that are at least weakly a product of ability), making the view a non-starter.

Table 1 Scoreboard

	Gettier	Value of K	Temp	Chi-V	Fake barn	Dream	Total
Safe TB	✓	x	x	✓	?	?	✓ x x ✓ ? ?
ALVE	✓	x	✓	✓	?	?	✓ x ✓ ✓ ? ?
G-aptness	✓	✓	✓	?	x	✓	✓ ✓ ✓ ? x ✓
S-aptness	✓	✓	✓	✓	?	✓	✓ ✓ ✓ ✓ ? ✓

Here's a brief justification of these rankings, with reference to what we've discussed so far:

Knowledge as Safe True Belief

Full points (✓) for the Gettier problem, as Gettiered beliefs are un-(SC)-safe. A bad mark (x) for the value of knowledge, as swamping-style arguments can be run against this account just as easily as against reliabilism.[36] Also, a bad mark (x) is clearly warranted for the TEMP case, which is designed to attack the sufficiency of safe, true, belief for knowledge. The safe, true belief view gets full points (✓) again for CHICAGO VISITOR – nothing problematic here; that said, the view rules out knowledge in FAKE BARN; I've given the middle ranking (?) of 'dubious/unclear' however, because, for one thing, the view relies on SC-safety which (as we've just seen) implies at best dubious results about dream scepticism. But also, given that what counts as 'getting it right' is unclear in the FAKE BARN case, it is also contentious that ruling out knowledge is the right result. Finally, the view gets a generous mark of dubious/unclear (?) in the case of dreaming scepticism. I've argued that a friend of SC-safety has no excellent response to dream scepticism. However, the third of the strategies considered – which appeals to external bases, ceding no assumptions to the sceptic – was shown to be less attractive than AAA-safety, though not clearly a bad strategy. Thus, a mark of dubious/unclear vis-à-vis dream scepticism. Total: ✓ x x ✓ ? ?

(ALVE) Knowledge = Safe, True Belief (SC) + (WACK)

This view gets assessed exactly the same as the safe true belief view, with one key exception: the view gets a strong (✓) score in the case of TEMP, rather than a bad score – as the weak ability condition WACK is strong enough to rule out Temp as knowing in that case. It's worth pointing out that the ability condition, WACK, we saw, was not so strong as to face the kind of difficulties (viz., to do

---

[36] Though, for an alternative approach to swamping, compare Hetherington 2018.

with defending abilities as most causally salient in explaining the recipient's success) that Greco-aptness faces in CHICAGO VISITOR, and so ALVE's inclusion of a weak safety condition does not block it from getting full marks in vindicating testimonial knowledge. Total: ✓ x ✓ ✓ ? ?

Knowledge = Greco-Aptness

This view, we've seen, gets off to a very strong start. It gets full marks for the Gettier problem (✓) *and* it's tailor made to address the Value of Knowledge (✓). Given that the *way* the view resolves the Gettier problem is not through a modal codicil but through an ability condition, the view has no problems with the TEMP case, thus full marks (✓) here as well. We looked at length at how the knowledge = Greco-aptness view addresses CHICAGO VISITOR. Contrary to what critics such as Lackey and Pritchard have held, Greco's response is not flawed in an intractable way. That said, and contrary to Greco, we saw that the response remains at best dubious/unclear (?) – given the dialectical burden that comes with Greco's commitment to explanatory salience. As for FAKE BARN, Greco's response here is, I've suggested, problematic even taking into account that what verdict we should give in FAKE BARN cases is contentious. Greco, we saw, paid a high price to get the result that one lacks knowledge in fake barn cases, and that price was to invite what we called the Overgeneralisation Argument. Given this unavoidable and serious problem, knowledge = Greco-aptness gets, for FAKE BARN, its first bad mark (x): it pays a large price for a minimal gain. Finally, because Greco-aptness rules out lucky beliefs in Gettier cases without signing up to SC-safety, it does not incur the problems that face SC-safety endorsing views when it comes to the nearness of the dreaming scenario. Thus, there's no good cause to dock points here (✓). Total: ✓ ✓ ✓ ? x ✓

Knowledge = Sosa-Aptness

The view that knowledge = Sosa-aptness starts strong and stays strong. There is no problem with standard Gettier cases like SHEEP IN THE FIELD. Roddy's belief is accurate and adroit, but not accurate *because* adroit (✓). Moreover, like the view that knowledge = Greco-aptness and *unlike* ALVE, the connection between ability and success is strong enough to imply that Sosa-apt beliefs will be cognitive achievements – and thus, we get full marks (✓) for the value of knowledge. Like *both* ALVE and the view that knowledge = Greco-aptness but unlike the view that knowledge = safe, true, belief, the view that knowledge = Sosa-aptness has no trouble explaining why knowledge is *not* present in TEMP (✓); the reason is that the correctness of Temp's belief does not manifest competence – his belief, while SC-safe, is thus not apt. The view *also* gets full marks (✓) for CHICAGO VISITOR – as was argued, the *sense* in which Sosa-apt beliefs are achievements creditable to the subject requires only that the correctness of one's belief manifest (complete) competence; this is something we can vindicate in testimony cases like CHICAGO VISITOR without needing to take a stand on any comparative claim (as Greco must do) about the contribution of the recipient *versus the informant* to the recipient's success. What about FAKE BARN? The dialectic around this kind of case was of course complex. Sosa-apt belief is – unlike for all three competitor views canvassed – *attributed* in this case. Although this came at what appeared initially to be the theoretical cost of rejecting SC-safety, that cost under closer inspection was not so high at all. On the contrary, we saw, there are advantages to SSS-safety over SC-safety. Thus, from what we've seen, the friend of knowledge = Sosa-aptness does not 'lose points' simply for rejecting SC-safety in its diagnosis of FAKE BARN. The view more than equalises any apparent loss here once SSS-safety and SC-safety are compared. *Nonetheless*, the view that knowledge = Sosa-aptness shouldn't receive full marks for its diagnosis of FAKE BARN. Although the view was shown to do better than Greco's view (the friend of knowledge = Sosa-aptness, after all, avoids the overgeneralisation argument) – it remains *no better*, from what we've said thus far, than either ALVE or the safe, true, belief view, which diagnosed FAKE BARN as a case where knowledge is *lacking*. As noted, it remains highly controversial (unlike in standard Gettier cases) whether FAKE BARN is a case of knowledge or not, and both champions of knowledge = Sosa-aptness *and* their opponents who rule out knowledge in FAKE BARN via SC-safety offer nothing to assuage opposing intuitions. Thus, an imperfect mark of 'dubious/unclear' (?) for the knowledge = Sosa-aptness proponent in FAKE BARN. By contrast, as we've elaborated on in some detail, from the idea that knowledge requires aptness (and thus SSS-safety) rather than SC-safety, we have no problems vindicating perceptual knowledge in the good case even if the dreaming scenario is modally close; so, full marks here. (✓), and an advantage for SSS-safety implied by aptness over SC-safety. Total: ✓ ✓ ✓ ✓ ? ✓

Appendix: Analysing Knowledge: A Sisyphean Folly?

This appendix aims to rebut an anticipated methodological challenge on behalf of the *knowledge-first* paradigm in epistemology, introduced through Williamson's *Knowledge and Its Limits*. In the book's opening chapter, Williamson argues that analysing knowledge in terms of constituent components is a fool's errand, one we should give up on. So do Williamson's arguments against analysing knowledge succeed in undercutting the motivation for the present project?

My take is as follows. Unlike some philosophers who have tried to maintain that Williamson's argumentation (either his Negative Abduction Argument[37] or his Distinct Concepts Argument[38]) against analysing knowledge is deeply flawed – I want to instead *grant* the thrust of both of these arguments and challenge their *scope*: they don't extend so far as to undermine the motivation for analysing knowledge as apt belief, even if these arguments throw a spanner in other kinds of attempts.

The Negative Abduction Argument

Early on in *Knowledge and its Limits*, a datum that Williamson (2000) draws attention to, and reasons from, is the alleged 'failure of the extensive post-Gettier research programme over several decades' (434). The narrative he presents is a familiar one: we find that 'a succession of increasingly complex analyses have been overturned by increasingly complex counterexamples' (Williamson 2000, 31). The trend towards complexity in these accounts (and their counterexamples) is such that Williamson takes it to reveal 'obvious signs of a *degenerating research program*. Most of them [the analyses of knowledge], if correct, seemed to make knowledge too grue-like to be worth analyzing' (2; my italics).

Williamson is, in the these passages, effectively drawing an inference (from a particular type of ostensibly unfruitful track record achieved by a methodological strategy) to the purported best explanation of that track record – viz., that the methodological strategy manifest in the bad track record is flawed. There is nothing wrong with this kind of negative abduction argument generally. It is an instance of the type: 'Method X has failed many/most/all times in the past' (is evidence for) 'X is a failure as a method'.

Moreover, this kind of negative abduction looks compelling when we reflect on the kind of highly complex analyses we find as representative in epistemology in the several decades after the 1960s.[39] The *method* characteristically used in these decades (and which Williamson rightly takes objection to) is 'conquer through increasing complexity', where increasing complexity was taken to be what was needed to address previous less complex but extensionally inadequate analyses.

However, shortly after Williamson's negative abduction against knowledge analyses in *KAIL* in 2000, early versions of the virtue epistemologist's core idea – that knowledge is type-identical with apt belief – were beginning to take

---

[37] For criticism of the Negative Abduction Argument, see Gerken 2018; and Hetherington 2016.

[38] For criticism of Williamson's DCA, see Goldman 2009; and Cassam 2009. For discussion, see Otero 2020.

[39] For an overview, see Shope 1983.

shape.[40] Identifying knowledge with apt belief is not a continuation of a pattern of more complex, artificial views. In its simplicity it represents a reversal of that trend. Negative abduction from failures of a methodology of increasingly complex analyses to the failure of a *simple* analysis is not justified. Accordingly, then, even if the Negative Abduction Argument is bad news for gerrymandered analyses, this bad news doesn't obviously extend to the idea that knowledge is apt belief, or to simple variations on this idea.

The Distinct Concepts Argument

Williamson has another argument, though. This one doesn't rely on abduction from a bad track record, but instead directly challenges *any* analysis of the concept of knowledge that equates KNOWLEDGE with a certain kind of conjunctive concept. Here's how the argument goes:

Distinct Concepts Argument
1. Every standard analysis of the concept knows equates it with some conjunctive concept which has the concept TRUE as a non-redundant constituent.
2. The concept TRUE is not a mental concept.
3. Any concept with a non-redundant non-mental constituent is not a mental concept.
4. So the conjunctive concepts with which the concept knows is equated by analyses of the standard kind are not mental concepts.
5. The concept KNOWS is a mental concept.
6. A mental concept can't be the very same concept as a non-mental concept.
7. So the mental concept KNOWS can't be the same concept as any of the conjunctive concepts with which it is equated by standard analyses.
8. So every standard analysis of the concept KNOWS is incorrect.[41]

As with the Negative Abduction Argument, the Distinct Concepts Argument is effective against *some* analyses, but not against the analysis *type* distinctive of virtue epistemology. To see why, we can set aside the question of whether the identification of knowledge and apt belief is centrally a *metaphysical analysis*[42] (which I take to be right) as opposed to *merely* a *conceptual* analysis. Let's assume for the sake of argument the metaphysical claim is at

---

[40] The first versions of this thesis are found in the early to mid 1990s (see Sosa 1991; Zagzebski 1996) Sosa (2007) further develops it substantially.

[41] I borrow this particular way of formulating Williamson's argument from Section 1.3 in KAIL from Cassam (2009). See also Sosa 2015, n. 13.

[42] For discussion, see Carter and Sosa 2021; Sosa 2015, chapter 1).

least accompanied with the equating of the concept KNOWLEDGE with the concept APT BELIEF.

Even granting this, the Distinct Concepts Argument doesn't threaten the kind of proposal we're pursuing. This is because (*contra* P1) *not all*, analyses of KNOWS involve *irredundant* non-mental component concepts. Williamson's argument is inapplicable to such accounts. The Distinct Concepts Argument is *inapplicable*, for instance, to Brian Ball's (2013) account of knowledge as normal belief. It is also inapplicable to Goldman's (1967) account of knowledge as belief caused by the fact believed. Neither equate the concept KNOWS with some conjunctive concept which has the concept TRUE as a non-redundant constituent. And neither, crucially for our purposes, does the analysis of knowledge as apt belief (as belief whose correctness manifests the believer's relevant competence).[43]

A Positive Motivation

In sum, because the identification of knowledge with apt belief is neither (i) a complex or gerrymandered analysis; nor (ii) does it involve any irredundant non-mental component concepts, neither of Williamson's arguments for thinking analyses of knowledge are unpromising are applicable to the view that knowledge is apt belief.

What is more, there is a *positive* methodological reason for thinking that a knowledge = apt belief analysis would be promising. Consider that one of the most beguiling problems that crops up in analyses of broadly factive phenomena (knows, acts, perceives, etc.) is the problem of *deviant causation*. This problem naturally leads analyses to be complex.

However, as Miracchi and Carter (2022) note, the 'X is apt Y' analysis schema allows us to avoid unnecessarily complicated analyses (including, via complications to do with deviant causation) across a wide range of broadly factive phenomena *F* – viz., phenomena *F* that entail success conditions that are possibly not met by a given *F*-attempt. To give a few more examples: Miracchi (2017) and Sosa (2015, chapter 1) hold that perception is apt perceptual experience. Sosa holds that action is apt intention. Miracchi and Carter (2022) hold that that understanding is apt conception. Each of these theories (perception is apt perceptual experience, action is apt intention, understanding is apt conception) uses aptness to 'connect' a given attempt-type with its corresponding (factive) realisation.

The thesis that knowledge = apt belief can, accordingly, be appreciated as an instance of a promising analysis-pattern, one that has advantages elsewhere, as

---

[43] For discussion, see Sosa 2015, n. 13.

opposed to an instance of a type that we should be sceptical would work (e.g., a gerrymandered analysis, or an analysis that identifies the concept KNOWS with some conjunctive concept which has the concept TRUE as a non-redundant constituent.)

This should lead us to be prima facie optimistic rather than pessimistic about the knowledge = apt belief template. Defending a virtue-epistemological analysis of knowledge is not in bad company with other strategies of analysis that we should rightly be suspicious of.

2 Virtue Epistemology: Two Levels Is Even Better

So far we've seen that the (uni-level) view that knowledge is type-identical to Sosa-aptness is able to accomplish quite a bit. And yet, we should have at least some reservations about the proposal nonetheless: being better than the competition thus far is a strike in favour of a view. But once we hold the view up to more demanding standards, we start to see some further chinks in the armour, and ones that it's not clear how (continuing to traffic within the confines of uni-level epistemology) we can address satisfactorily.

Here is the plan for this section. We begin by pressing the uni-level knowledge = Sosa-aptness view on two critical points, to do with (i) fake barns; and (ii) coherence and rationality.

We'll then introduce one (albeit, important) piece of machinery to the view we've got so far – the *animal/reflective knowledge distinction*, which will come close to dealing with both issues. To a first approximation (which will be superseded) this distinction lines up with the intuitive gain we make when moving from *knowing* something (animal knowledge) and *knowing that you know it* (reflective knowledge).[44]

What exactly is the *price,* though, of stratifying knowledge into two grades, one corresponding with *mere* knowledge, the other knowledge knowledgeably held? Kornblith thinks it is far too high. We'll consider his reasoning in the form of two main arguments: the *proliferation argument* and the *reliability argument*. Neither argument, we'll see, is sound. However, responding to the reliability argument will reveal an important way in which we should distinguish (beyond what Sosa has) between *multiple types of reflective knowledge* – what I call *descriptive* and *predictive* reflective knowledge – as well as distinguishing them both from what Sosa calls *knowledge full well*, which marks his attempt to 'replace' reflective knowledge on the top of the epistemic hill.

---

[44] Note that the animal/reflective distinction marks one kind of hierarchical picture of knowledge, albeit not the only one. For a different kind of hierarchical picture, one that countenances grades of knowledge (albeit not via an animal/reflective distinction), see Hetherington (e.g., in 2001 and 2011, Sections 2.6–2.8).

By this point in the section, we'll have a more sophisticated, stratified picture of knowledge that is more powerful than the simple 'knowledge = apt belief' idea we began with; and we will see how this revised, stratified picture of knowledge forces some corresponding revisions elsewhere in our core triad (viz., the corresponding normative kind thesis and cognitive achievement thesis).

Even though this new and improved picture can withstand Kornblith's criticisms, there remain two important loose ends. One concerns how our perceptual knowledge can be vindicated as high-grade (and not merely animal knowledge) given the nearness of the dreaming scenario. This challenge, we'll see, can be met with the resources from this section. Second, we consider a final problem – what I'll call the *performance granularity problem*. The performance granularity problem remains intractable on the present picture and requires some new ideas to address – which will then set the scene for the next section.

2.1 FAKE BARN, Redux

Remember on our working scoreboard, the simple view that knowledge = Sosa-aptness didn't quite get full marks; despite boasting a better diagnosis of FAKE BARN than critics such as Pritchard have given the view credit for, the view still was said to offer a 'dubious/unclear' diagnosis of the problem. Let's look again at *why*, and what would be needed to do better.

Because the matter of whether the subject *knows* in a fake barn case is contentious (knowledge = Sosa-aptness says 'yes') – a fully satisfactory diagnosis of FAKE BARN should offer at least some kind of error theory that can help us to make sense of the venerable tradition that holds that (i) knowledge isn't present in such cases, because (ii) SC-safety fails.

Although the simple view that knowledge = Sosa-aptness was shown to be capable of satisfactorily *defending itself* against the charge that it gives up safety altogether simply by attributing knowledge in FAKE BARN, we don't yet have any explanation for why so many have found the other side so attractive. If (as the view holds) knowledge requires *only* SSS-safety but not SC-safety, then why have so many epistemologists drawn a line in the sand around SC-safety, with some (like Pritchard) going so far as to take SC-safety to be a bedrock platitude?

It's not clear what more uni-level virtue epistemology, on which knowledge = Sosa-aptness can say at this point. With one level of knowledge to work with, the friend of knowledge = Sosa-aptness has already left all its resources on the field defending itself as not having a bad diagnosis of FAKE BARN; there's not obviously any more resources left to offer any kind of error theory to the competition.

2.2 Broad Coherence?

A second kind of worry about (uni-level) knowledge = Sosa-aptness is that it lacks any obvious way to explain why coherence in our beliefs is valuable.

First, some background. There's a good reason we've not taken seriously thus far the idea that knowledge is true belief that satisfies a *coherentist* requirement – viz., that the belief coheres with other beliefs one has by standing in deductive, inductive, and explanatory support relations with these other beliefs.[45] The reason is that such a view has no serious prospects for addressing the Gettier problem, and as such, it's a non-starter qua analysis of knowledge.[46] Even more, *coherence* can't be all there is to epistemic justification; if it *were*, then it becomes very difficult to say why our beliefs are any more justified than the beliefs of the conspiracy theorist whose conspiracy theory is internally consistent and self-supporting. This is all well-trodden territory.[47]

Even so, it would be an error to reason from these points to the conclusion that broad coherence in one's beliefs lacks *any* epistemic value. And this is so even if apt belief – knowledge, on the view we've been working with so far – doesn't require it. Just consider: a thinker who starts piling up apt beliefs via apt competence exercise does better when using reason to see connections between these beliefs, and to (through track record evidence) come to appreciate their beliefs as reliably sourced. But *why* should any such appreciation, that broad coherence surely contributes to, boost in any way the value of a belief when the belief can be *known* (through merely apt exercise of competence) without it? The simple view that knowledge = Sosa-aptness offers no good guidance here.

2.3 Introducing Two Levels

Without further ado: the key idea, which we'll see brings with it just the payoffs we need to address both the residual issues noted (concerning fake barns and coherence, respectively) is to distinguish between – to a first approximation, for now – apt belief *simpliciter* and apt belief *aptly noted* – viz., apt belief that the subject aptly believes to be apt.

The former is what Sosa calls *animal knowledge*, the latter *reflective knowledge*. For simplicity in reference, if we use K to designate animal knowledge (i.e., apt belief) and K^+ to designate reflective knowledge (i.e., apt belief aptly believed to be apt), then we distinguish two grades of knowledge as follows:

---

[45] For discussion, see Littlejohn and Carter 2021.

[46] Though, for a different take on the status of the Gettier problem as a kind of adequacy criterion, see Hetherington 2016.

[47] For some discussions of this objection, see Littlejohn and Carter 2021; see also Sosa 1980, 1997.

Two grades of knowledge: animal and reflective

- **Animal knowledge**: S has animal knowledge (K) that p iff S beliefs p aptly.
- **Reflective knowledge**: S has reflective knowledge K^+ that p iff S believes aptly that S believes p aptly. That is: $K^+(p) \leftrightarrow K(K(p))$.

The terms 'animal' and 'reflective' (which Sosa originally coined) aren't especially important for our purposes. What is important is that what we've been calling *knowledge* (i.e., Sosa-apt belief) so far now occupies a place in a *hierarchy*, below reflective knowledge. Reflective knowledge asymmetrically entails animal knowledge; it is more demanding epistemically.

Whereas animal knowledge needn't be *defensibly* apt (the thinker simply needs to get it right through competence), reflective knowledge does. The reflective knower (by having animal knowledge that their belief is apt and thus animal knowledge) is in a position to defend that knowledge against sceptical doubts.

Before showing how we can put the animal/reflective distinction to work, it will be helpful to quickly register that, by rejecting the uni-level thesis, we are in effect now revising the CKT, as well as the two other theses that form part of the core triad – namely, the normative kind and cognitive achievement theses, as follows:

Revised Core Triad (Bi-level Virtue Epistemology)

- **Revised core knowledge thesis (CKT*)**: Propositional knowledge is apt belief – either mere apt belief (animal knowledge) or apt belief aptly noted (reflective knowledge).
- **Revised normative kind thesis (NKT*)**: Knowledge is a normative kind; qua normative kind, it is a genus with two species: animal knowledge and reflective knowledge.
- **Revised cognitive achievement thesis (CAT*)**: Knowledge is a (species of) cognitive achievement, with a hierarchy of grades: reflective knowledge is a higher-grade achievement than animal knowledge.

Let's now see how this (revised) core triad offers some straightforward ways to improve upon what was already a strong view (knowledge = Sosa-aptness) by offering new ways to address each of the limitations to the view we've highlighted – viz., concerning (i) fake barns; and (ii) the place of coherence.

2.4 FAKE BARN: The Full Error Theory

Here were the two main questions that were left unanswered for the proponent of (uni-level) knowledge = Sosa-aptness:

- *Q1*: What might explain why epistemologists are often disinclined to attribute knowledge in FAKE BARN, even though (as we've seen) there are good reasons to think knowledge requires just SSS-safety and not SC-safety (which would rule out knowledge in these cases)?
- *Q2*: Relatedly, what explains the intuition – held by many epistemologists – that knowledge generally requires SC-safety (not met in FAKE BARN) and not just SSS-safety of the sort present in FAKE BARN?

With two levels to work with, we now have an error theory that addresses both questions in one swoop. The answer to Q1 is that there *really is* valuable kind of human knowledge lacking in FAKE BARN and which *does* require much more than just achieving SSS-safety. When one has reflective knowledge, one's belief is *not* going to be *luckily apt*, as it is in FAKE BARN. Whereas animal knowledge, which requires just SSS-safety, is compatible with the SSS-conditions holding unsafely, reflective knowledge requires that *not easily* would the (reflectively known) belief have failed to be apt, and thus, that the SSS conditions do not hold unsafely.[48]

In response to Q2: the attractiveness to SC-safety can be explained in our bi-level view by pointing to the fact that there is an epistemic standing *in the neighbourhood of (animal) knowledge*, which really does require not just SSS-safety, but SC-safety. The opponent's mistake is to think that *all* knowledge requires this.

These answers to Q1 and Q2 – which the addition of the animal/reflective distinction offers us – take us beyond the kind of diagnosis of FAKE BARN we were able to muster by the end of Section 1. We now have at our disposal a view that can *not only* defend itself satisfactorily against the charge that it problematically awards knowledge in a way that runs contrary to SC-safety (this we had by the end of Section 1); but which can *also* show how the flew can accommodate the intuitions driving that charge.

2.5 The Place of Coherence in Virtue Epistemology

Whereas a uni-level virtue epistemology was shown to risk (like other forms of externalism in epistemology[49]) marginalising entirely the place of broad coherence in a theory of knowledge, our two-tiered picture allows us to see how it can add value to the knowledge we have. And this is so even though, on any kind of virtue epistemology, the conspiracy theorist's web of unreliably sourced but coherent beliefs gives them not even justification.

---

[48] This is Sosa's position on the animal/reflective knowledge distinction from roughly 2007–21; *Epistemic Explanations* (2021) marks a newer shift in Sosa's thinking about this distinction, and whether SC-safety would be implicated by reflective knowledge.

[49] Compare, however, Pritchard's (in press) moderate externalism.

How so? Consider that while animal knowledge doesn't require the subject to have any epistemic perspective on the target belief, *reflective knowledge does* require such a perspective.[50] Remember: reflective knowledge requires, at the *second order*, an *apt* belief that your first order belief is apt. Aptness, at any order, requires competence; and competence at the second order (by which one can when all goes well aptly believe their belief to be apt) is a competence we can clearly improve through coherence-seeking inferential reasoning, reasoning by which we can appreciate (for a given belief) that if correct its correctness would manifest ability, that it would be apt. This is the case even though one's initially possessing animal knowledge needn't be explained by any coherent body of beliefs in one's command.

The wider explanation that the incorporation of an animal/reflective knowledge distinction affords the virtue epistemologist for vindicating the place of broad coherence in a theory of knowledge can then be framed in a simple analogy with memory: if our *first* order competences are given bad inputs, then coherence-seeking inferential reasoning (between these bad inputs to the reasoning) doesn't give us anything more valuable epistemically than we had before. This is akin to how if you *misremember* something (take in a bad input), then nothing is gained from the skilled retention of that memory and integration of the bad memory with one's other beliefs. However, the story is very different when we have good inputs: broad coherence, when combined with good inputs (e.g., the outputs of externally competent faculties) is valuable.

In this way, then, a bi-level virtue epistemology has an available story for the place of broad coherence in a theory of knowledge, which offers it an advantage on this score over uni-level externalist theories of knowledge, including the uni-level view that knowledge = Sosa-aptness, which would render the epistemic value of coherence mysterious.

2.6 Two Levels on the Defence: Challenges from Kornblith

Is adding this extra 'level' of knowledge somehow cheating? Have we got the goods here (e.g., in Sections 1.4–1.5) by theft rather than toil?

It's not at all clear that we have. The idea that different grades of knowledge that correspond with different levels of demandingness is not a new one at all. This core idea is already present in Descartes' epistemology: for Descartes, the lower level is termed *cognitio* and the higher-level *scientia;*[51] the ascent from

---

[50] See Sosa 2009, 2:135.

[51] While it is clear Descartes distinguished *cognitio* and *scientia*, it is debatable whether and to what extent this distinction lines up with features of Sosa's animal/reflective distinction. For a view that the similarity is a close one, see Sosa (2017, chapter 1).

lower to higher knowledge marks an intellectually valuable transition attained through reflection on one's epistemic position.[52]

But, of course, 'Descartes did it!' isn't an argument so much as just an instance of precedent. And at least some commentators have objected to the animal/reflective distinction as a viable move in one's epistemology. Let's turn now to two prominent arguments by Hilary Kornblith to this effect – the *proliferation argument* and the *reliability argument*.[53] The proliferation argument is a methodological objection; the reliability argument challenges the animal/reflective distinction by way of challenging the epistemic value of reflection. Neither argument, we'll see, succeeds in hitting its mark.

2.6.1 The Proliferation Argument

According to Kornblith, the animal/reflective distinction is not a justified distinction to draw in the theory of knowledge, in so far as it purports to pick out distinctive types of knowledge that are of epistemological interest. This general 'distinction without a difference' line has been given multiple spins in Kornblith's *On Reflection* (2012), including that (i) the distinction is unmotivated, or not worth drawing; and (ii) the distinction problematically overgeneralises to other distinctions that are themselves not worth drawing.

This section has already offered a basis from which to rebut (i). The distinction is worth drawing because, by drawing it, a view of knowledge (at least, a particular view on which knowledge = Sosa-aptness) can deliver more goods than it can otherwise. We thus have good *pro tanto* reason to draw the distinction.

That said, the second spin on the 'distinction without a difference' worry – that it implies the *proliferation of unworthy distinctions* among knowledge types – requires further response. Here's the basic structure of the argument, which uses the consultative/non-consultative knowledge quasi-distinction for *reductio*.

Proliferation argument
1. Animal and reflective knowledge are different kinds of knowledge only if consultative and non-consultative knowledge are different kinds of knowledge.

---

[52] For a discussion here, see Sosa 2017, chapter 1); and Reed 2002. In Descartes' epistemology, this distinction is applicable in, for example, the case of the atheist mathematician. See Descartes 2002, 101. A distinction between higher and lower knowledge is also drawn by Wang Yangming; see Lederman 2020.

[53] For critical discussion see also Carter and McKenna 2019; compare Perrine 2014.

2. Consultative and non-consultative knowledge are not different kinds of knowledge.
3. Therefore, it's not the case that animal and reflective knowledge are different kinds of knowledge.

Consultative knowledge, as Kornblith construes it, is knowledge you gain from the process of consulting with people (say, a group of friends), something that *can* of course potentially help improve the epistemic status of your belief.

We can grant Kornblith (2012) that countenancing consultative and non-consultative knowledge as distinct kinds of epistemological interest *simply on the basis of their deriving from different processes* 'multiplies kinds of knowledge far beyond necessity' (19). That said, notice that Kornblith's support for Premise 1 relies on the basis of the distinction between animal and reflective knowledge being drawn with reference to *processes* that a thinker has 'gone through' in attaining the relevant knowledge (where the process taken to be distinctive of reflective knowledge is the process of reflection).[54]

Let's grant Kornblith that a good basis for drawing a distinction between *natural kinds* N_1 and N_2 is not going to be that N_1 and N_2 were arrived at through different processes. There is no natural kind distinction that tracks a difference between gold attained by the process of mining versus the process of using a metal detector. If knowledge were assumed to be a *natural kind*, then, there we should not expect differences in knowledge kinds to track differences in processes involved in knowledge realisation.[55]

But knowledge, on our view, is *not* a natural kind. Recall again one of the components of the wider package that has thus far largely flown under the radar: knowledge is a *normative kind*, distinguished not by what distinguishes natural kinds (intrinsic properties) but by what distinguishes other normative kinds, and this can include (non-intrinsic) relational properties. Animal knowledge is type-identical not with any psychological state-type but with *apt* belief (where aptness picks out a normative standing), reflective knowledge is apt belief aptly noted (a different normative standing, normatively superior to mere aptness). The *basis* for drawing this distinction is thus not merely (like with the consultative/non-consultative knowledge quasi-distinction) the process that brought it about, as such, but its normative standing, qua aimed performance.

The foregoing allows us to better see what might have led Kornblith astray: he overlooks that the animal/reflective knowledge distinction is not drawn *on the basis of* the latter arising through a process of reflection and the former not (a distinction ill-suited to differentiate *natural* kinds) but on the basis of the two

---

[54] For criticism on this point, see Perrine 2014.   [55] For discussion, see Bird 2008.

occupying different normative standings (a difference that would suffice to differentiate *normative* kinds).

2.6.2 The Reliability Argument

Let's consider another line of argument that Kornblith has levelled against the animal/reflective knowledge distinction, and which targets the view (implicit in our revised achievement thesis) that reflective knowledge is *superior* to animal knowledge. Here is the simple template formulation of the reasoning:

Reliability argument

1. Reflective knowledge is superior to animal knowledge only if reflection produces more reliable beliefs.
2. Reflection does not produce more reliable beliefs.
3. Therefore, reflective knowledge is not superior to animal knowledge.[56]

Kornblith takes it that Premise 1 is more or less obvious and that Premise 2 – which challenges the reliability of reflection – is where the action lies.

There is more than a little space to quibble with Premise 1 – and we'll circle back to some of these reasons, which are important. But to engage with Kornblith charitably, let's grant Premise 1 for the sake of argument and think a bit about Premise 2.

Whether Premise 2 is true, as Kornblith (2012) rightly notes, is subject to empirical refutation (or confirmation), and he offers some empirical evidence that he thinks shows that reflection does not generally increase reliability (20–6).

First, we are generally bad at identifying the causes of our beliefs. Many of our belief-forming processes occur below the level of consciousness.[57] Second, when we try to identify the relevant processes, we often make mistakes because our beliefs are influenced by factors we mistakenly treat as irrelevant. For instance, Kornblith discusses evidence that suggests that our judgements about the reliability and trustworthiness of politicians are influenced by the colours of their campaign materials in ways that can't be explained by political colour-coding (e.g., red = left wing). Third, when we reflect on our beliefs, we often end up rationalising them rather than uncovering these problems.

---

[56] I borrow this formulation of Perrine (2014, 253). For a related argument, see Kornblith 2012, 26–34; compare Carter and McKenna 2019, 5002.

[57] This point gains support from empirical work on heuristics and biases, but also on empirical work in cognitive science which distinguishes subpersonal processes as playing causally important roles in explaining cognition. See, e.g., Drayson 2014.

As Kornblith (2012) puts it: 'In a large class of cases, the process of reflection is an exercise in self-congratulation. It does nothing, however, in these important cases, to improve on the accuracy of our first-order beliefs' (25).

Kornblith's claim is that the empirical evidence suggests that reflection generally fails to increase the reliability of our reasoning. In response, it's probably fair to complain that Kornblith overstates the strength of the empirical evidence. For example, Declan Smithies (2011) has recently drawn attention to several examples of cases where reflection can and does increase the reliability of our reasoning. This is the case, for example, in both logical reasoning[58] and moral reasoning,[59] among other areas.[60]

If we adjudicate the question of the reliability of reflection empirically, as Kornblith suggests, it looks like the result is that the jury is out rather than that reflection is generally unreliable. But – and this brings us to a point that bears on both P1 and P2 of the argument – the *reliability of reflection* (of the sort that we might learn about by appealing to empirical studies) is really *irrelevant* to whether reflective knowledge is superior to animal knowledge. So it doesn't matter whether the jury is out on the empirical point (or the empirical jury stands in Kornblith's favour).

This is because the picture we are working with does not take *reflection* to be capable *in and of itself* of doing anything special at all. Pointing out that reflection alone is not great (in the ways Kornblith says), accordingly, is not a direct challenge to the kind of two-tiered picture of knowledge we're working with.

'Reflective knowledge' is a term of art that refers to something very specific: a belief that is not only apt but *meta-apt* – viz., such that its aptness is aptly grasped. Reflective knowledge is not secured by having an apt belief *that one simply reflects upon* thereby increasing its epistemic status and/or value. If *that* were the view, then it would indeed stand in the crosshairs of Kornblith's reliability argument.

P1, then, is false. It is not the case that reflective knowledge is superior to animal knowledge only if some claim is true about the reliability of beliefs formed by reflection; but rather, only if apt beliefs aptly grasped are superior to apt beliefs.

2.7 Reflective Knowledge: A Conundrum

The introduction of an animal/reflective distinction into the picture developed so far doesn't succumb to either of the Kornblith-style arguments we just considered. That's good. But we're not off the hook yet.

---

[58] See Gagne et al. 1962.   [59] Small, Loewenstein, and Slovic 2007.
[60] See Pennebaker 2011; and Carter and McKenna 2019.

In this section, I want to lay out what I take to be an overlooked tension within our working view of reflective knowledge to this point, at least as it's been developed by Sosa. I'll then offer a new interpretation of the reflective level that can help us to resolve the tension.

One way of putting the tension in the spotlight is to think about two 'jobs' that – by Sosa's lights – *reflective knowledge* (at least, as we've described it so far, as *apt belief aptly noted*) is supposed to do. We'll see that the kind of thing reflective knowledge would need to *be* to do one job would actually *prevent* it from doing the other, and vice versa. This observation will set the scene for the distinction in reflective knowledge types we'll need to draw.

Let's call the first job for reflective knowledge 'DEFENCE'. Suppose you believe some perceptual belief, *p*, aptly. By virtue of being apt, the belief attains the status of animal knowledge, on our working view, even if you have no perspective at all on the reliability of the process that brought it about. Were a sceptic to challenge the matter of *whether* you know that *p*, you (equipped with mere animal knowledge that *p*) would be in the same position as any 'brute' externalist might be: you *do know* in virtue of possessing an apt belief, but lacking an (apt) conception of how your belief derived from competence (viz., something we've seen broad coherence in one's beliefs can help contribute to), you don't know *that*. You aren't in a position to knowledgeably defend your (animal) knowledge against sceptical doubts.

One of the claimed selling points of reflective knowledge, for Sosa, is that it arms you with exactly such a defence. Here's Sosa:

> [U]nderstand 'animal' knowledge as requiring apt belief without requiring defensibly apt belief, i.e., apt belief that the subject aptly believes to be apt, and whose aptness the subject can therefore defend against relevant skeptical doubts; and . . . understand 'reflective' knowledge as requiring not only apt belief but also defensibly apt belief.

Of course, reflective knowledge is going to be up to the job description of (DEFENCE) only if it is understood to be *knowledge about (already) possessed (animal) knowledge*. And that is exactly how reflective knowledge was initially described by Sosa (e.g., 2007) in the simple $K^+(p) \leftrightarrow K(K(p))$ formula. DEFENCE is probably the most important job description for reflective knowledge up until about 2010, when Sosa shifted focus to a different job for reflective knowledge, which we can call 'PERFORMANCE UPGRADE'.

In getting a grip on the importance of PERFORMANCE UPGRADE, just remember that, at the very core of the framework we're working with, epistemic normativity is a species of performance normativity. Epistemic evaluations (accuracy, adroitness, aptness) are all performance evaluations. Bearing this in mind, consider the following case pair:

HINDSIGHT-1: Steph is barely within his threshold for sufficient reliability to shoot aptly but doesn't know this. He shoots and makes it aptly. Even so (and not knowing he was so near the limit of his competence) his shot would very easily have been *inapt*. Afterwards, Steph studies the tape, and comes to know (i.e., aptly believe) that his shot on that occasion was apt.

HINDSIGHT-2: Steph* is barely within his threshold (100 metres) for aptly spotting a chaffinch, but doesn't know this. From here, he forms the belief (aptly) that there is a chaffinch. Even so (and not knowing he was so near the limit of his chaffinch-spotting competence) he very easily would have believed *inaptly*. Later that day, Steph* after consulting an eye doctor and statistician who have been keeping track of the distances from which Steph is reliable at spotting birds, he comes to know (i.e., aptly believe) that his belief on that occasion was apt.

It's obvious that, in HINDSIGHT-1, Steph's post-game study of the tape *doesn't make the shot he took during the game any better quality*. It doesn't increase the quality of the shot he took to later come to know that the shot was apt (which he didn't know at the time). The performance quality remains the same: merely apt, *and* such that (it's still the case that it) very easily it would have been inapt. It thus remains *luckily apt* (indeed, known to be so).

What goes for HINDSIGHT-1 goes for the epistemic variation HINDSIGHT-2. Steph's* consultation with the eye doctor and statistician doesn't make his performance better 'after the fact'. It remains that *that performance* was luckily apt.

There is, for Sosa, a way that Steph (and Steph*) *could* have increased the quality of their performances beyond mere aptness. But it's not by learning *later* that their performances were apt (even if learning *that* is helpful against the sceptic!). Rather, it's by doing two key things: for reference, call these *risk assessment* and *level connection*.

- *Risk assessment*: The performer can improve the quality of the performance by aptly assessing *that (the performance) would likely enough be apt*; and
- *Level connection*: When *risk assessment* is satisfied, the performer can improve the quality of the performance by performing aptly *because of* the apt second-order risk assessment.

Suppose *risk assessment* is satisfied in the basketball version of the case. Does *that* thereby improve the quality of Steph's (apt) shot? Not necessarily. It *could* contribute to doing so, but only if the risk assessment actually *influences* the shot in some way. (Consider: Steph *could* have satisfied *risk assessment* but then actually decided to take the shot by flipping a coin, making his risk assessment performatively idle.) In such a case, the apt risk assessment (at the second-order) is 'disconnected' from the apt performance at the first order.

Here's where *level connection* kicks in. If *that's* satisfied, then we can see how what one knows at the second order *really would* increase the quality of a given performance. If *risk assessment* and *level connection* are satisfied, then (say) a basketball shot will manifest not only good shooting technique but also *good shot selection* – and in a way that the apt shot *does not* in HINDSIGHT-1, where Steph would have easily shot inaptly. And mutatis mutandis, for HINDSIGHT-2.

From 2010 on, Sosa uses a new term to describe an apt performance the quality of which is upgraded by satisfying both *risk assessment* and *level connection* – its status is upgraded from *apt* to *fully apt*. Moreover, on this updated picture, when one satisfies risk assessment, then *regardless* of whether one's performance is fully apt, it is *meta-apt*.

The new picture featuring three grades of aptness accordingly looks like this:

Three grades of aptness
- **Aptness**: A performance is apt iff it is (first-order) accurate because adroit.
- **Meta-aptness**: A performance is meta-apt iff it corresponds with an apt second-order risk assessment that it would likely enough be apt.
- **Full aptness**: A performance is fully apt iff apt because meta-apt.

In the epistemic case in particular, the three levels of aptness correspond with three grades of knowledge: (1) aptness lines up with animal knowledge, (2) meta-aptness with reflective knowledge, and (3) full aptness with *knowledge full well*. As Sosa puts it:

> Apt belief, animal knowledge, is better than belief that succeeds in its aim, being true, without being apt. Apt belief aptly noted, reflective knowledge, is better than mere apt belief or animal knowledge, especially when the reflective knowledge helps to guide the first-order belief so that it is apt. In such a case the belief is fully apt, and the subject knows full well. (Sosa 2015, 93)

So on this new view, reflective knowledge (alternatively, on this updated picture, meta-apt belief) is valuable not only in its own right, but also in what it can *do:* it can help to guide a thinker to an apt belief at the first-order. When it does, you've got something even better than mere animal knowledge, or mere (animal + reflective knowledge), but you've got animal knowledge *because* of your reflective knowledge. Your reflective knowledge enables you to *upgrade* your first-order performance.

With this now all on the table, we're able to precisely state what looks like a real puzzle about reflective knowledge.

On the *one hand*, reflective knowledge is going to be up to the job description of DEFENCE only if understood to be *knowledge about (already) possessed (animal) knowledge*. On the other, reflective knowledge is going to be up to the job of PERFORMANCE UPGRADE only in so far as it is *predictive* in character – viz., only as knowledge that a given belief *would be* apt, and such that this risk assessment that features in the content of this knowledge actually influences (through *level connection*) one's believing, converting animal knowledge into knowledge full well. But – and here's the puzzle – reflective knowledge can't both (i) be knowledge about knowledge that *p* that one already has; and (ii) knowledge that could guide one to knowing that *p*. So, as the thought goes, reflective knowledge can't possibly do both jobs as advertised: DEFENCE and PERFORMANCE UPGRADE. If the content of reflective knowledge is *that one knows that p*, such reflective knowledge does will with DEFENCE but will fail PERFORMANCE UPGRADE. If the content of reflective knowledge is whether were one to believe *p* it would be apt, such reflective knowledge now is primed for meeting PERFORMANCE UPGRADE but will fail DEFENCE.

2.8 Reflective Knowledge Expanded

Should we simply give up reflective knowledge as incoherent, then? Hardly! In fact, this puzzle, while raising a problem for an interpretation of the stratified framework that tries to stretch reflective knowledge too thin to cover both DEFENCE and PERFORMANCE UPGRADE – at the same time – motivates the importance of doing both the jobs captured by DEFENCE and PERFORMANCE UPGRADE. We want our framework to have the horsepower to (i) defend animal knowledge against sceptical doubts, *and* we want to allow for knowledge to be upgraded via *risk assessment* and *level connection* in a way that is analogous to how other kinds of aimed performances can be similarly upgraded in quality this way.

The most straightforward way to get these results is to make a sharp and clear divorce between two *species* of reflective knowledge. Doing so will help to make our stratified picture clearer, *and* it will be easier to understand the benefits it offers. The key move is to simply distinguish the (i) content-type, (ii) psychological realisation, and (iii) performance-theoretic roles of:

Descriptive reflective knowledge: *S* has descriptive reflective knowledge iff for some proposition *p* that *S* aptly believes, *S* aptly believes that *S* aptly believes *p*.

Predictive (counterfactual) reflective knowledge: *S* has predictive (counterfactual) reflective knowledge iff for some proposition *p*, *S* aptly believes (or presupposes) that: were S to believe p, S's belief that p would (likely enough) be apt.

The (i) content-type of descriptive reflective knowledge is knowledge one already has. The psychological realisation of descriptive reflective knowledge requires occurrent belief (more on this shortly – this is a difference between the two types of reflective knowledge); and it requires this because an important *role* of this knowledge is characterised by DEFENCE. Historically, what we're calling descriptive reflective knowledge was the key and lone species of reflective knowledge (and DEFENCE the most important role) in Sosa's early virtue epistemology, where the benefit of broad coherence in defending knowledge against sceptical doubts was considered a central selling point of the bi-levelled picture.

The (i) content-type of predictive reflective knowledge is a counterfactual: were one to believe a proposition one would do so aptly. The psychological realisation of predictive reflective knowledge can be occurrent but needn't be; it can also be tacit and take the form of a presupposition. And the salient *role* of this knowledge (within the wider stratified framework) is characterised by its contribution to PERFORMANCE UPGRADE. Historically, what we're calling predictive reflective knowledge has been the most important species of reflective knowledge (and PERFORMANCE the most important role for reflective knowledge) in Sosa's more recent epistemology, which is centred around the idea that epistemic normativity is a species of performance normativity.

By distinguishing between these two species of reflective knowledge and the roles they play (and don't – and can't – play!) respectively, we get a clearer view of how stratified virtue epistemology gains specific results with reference to knowledge one has at the second order *of* first-order (i) possessed; and (ii) possible knowledge.

Working with this interpretation of reflective knowledge (and its place in the knowledge hierarchy), we're now in a position to update our core triad in a way that gives us the following new and improved working picture:

Revised Core Triad (Stratified Virtue Epistemology)

- **Revised core knowledge thesis (CKT**)**: Propositional knowledge is apt belief – either mere apt belief (animal knowledge) or meta-apt belief (either in the form of descriptive or prescriptive reflective knowledge) or fully apt belief (knowledge full well).
- **Revised normative kind thesis (NKT**)**: Knowledge is a normative kind; qua normative kind, it is a genus with three key species: aptness, meta-aptness, and full aptness.

- **Cognitive achievement thesis (CAT**)**: Knowledge is a (species of) cognitive achievement, with a hierarchy of grades – with knowledge full well (fully apt belief) at the top of the hierarchy.

Let's zoom out. This picture – characterised by our revised core triad – can explain a lot. It gets the benefits of the original (uni-level) 'knowledge = Sosa-aptness' view, but with *extra* benefits that the uni-level view couldn't offer: a fully satisfactory diagnosis of FAKE BARN and an advantage over typical externalist views in epistemology, which leave no clear explanation for the epistemic value added by broad coherence. We saw that the view holds up straightforwardly against stock objections (e.g., the proliferation argument and the reliability argument). In short, the 'knowledge = Sosa-aptness' view needed to pay the price of stratifying knowledge in order to get extra goods. But we've got good cause now to think that price was more than worth it.

We then saw that at least a simple version of the stratified picture, characterised by the formula $K^+(p) \leftrightarrow K(K(p))$, faced its own internal tensions. This was illustrated by drawing attention to the sense in which job descriptions DEFENCE and PERFORMANCE UPGRADE are mutually unsatisfiable. Our solution in this section has been a new interpretation of reflective knowledge that opts for a clean divorce between two species of reflective knowledge, each with its own explanatory benefits at the second-order.

Even so – our current working view still faces one residual problem, and it's one we can't fix with any simple tweak. We need to revisit, with a critical eye, the very idea of an aimed performance. We are after all, still working with the idea that performance normativity is applicable to beliefs in so far as beliefs are internally aimed at truth. This assumption, we'll see, raises a kind of problem we'll call the *performance granularity problem*. This problem will set the scene for the next section, which shows how Sosa addresses the problem, and then offers two substantive new improvements to his preferred solution.

3 Judgemental Knowledge: New Twists

This section will do three main things. First, in Section 3.1, we'll expand our framework to incorporate *stratified belief* into the picture developed so far, and in doing so, we'll see how some of Sosa's most recent moves offer a way to address (while raising some separate challenges) a problem to do with performance granularity.

The next two sections (Sections 3.2–3.3) then chart a new direction from Sosa in two key respects – both as regards how we should theorise about the structure of knowledge at the very highest grade (a template structure that will become clearer once *stratified belief* is incorporated into the picture).

Section 3.2 will focus on high-grade *level-connecting*: in slogan form, we are going to replace 'guidance' with 'basing' (as a level-connector), which will help to avoid certain kinds of counterexamples. Section 3.3 will then outline, critique, and replace Sosa's theory of what kinds of risk to (first-order) aptness a *fully apt* performer can non-negligently ignore. What we end up at the end of the section (and of this Element) will be a kind of stratified virtue epistemology that is a substantive refinement of the already powerful framework Sosa gives us.

3.1 From Stratified Knowledge to Stratified Belief

Consider that we believe many mundane things about our immediate environment, which guide action. This is so despite our having never attempted, through any conscious deliberation, to 'settle the question' for which an affirmation (i.e., on whether *p* – e.g., that the table is an arm's length away) would constitute an answer. Some of these beliefs are apt, as they will be when their correctness (i.e., truth) manifests competence. Others aren't.

But clearly not *all* our beliefs are like this. Not all of our beliefs seem to 'aim' *merely* at truth. Just think about when you take up the question of whether a friend has lied to you or whether a particular insurance policy will save you money in the long run. When undertaking such 'whether *p*' questions, we plausibly aim not *just* at getting it right any old way (as a quiz contestant might, by making a guess), but at affirming if and only if we do so *aptly*. That is, we *intentionally* aim at settling the whether-question with *apt belief – knowledge* – rather than at truth any old way. This is, by way of an athletic comparison, just as a basketball player, while sizing up whether to take a shot, aims not *merely* to make the shot any old way (as one might do when chucking a reckless three-pointer), but to *make it through competence.*

But if, as this suggests, some beliefs seem to aim at truth (and so are apt when that aim, the aim of *truth*, is aptly attained), and other beliefs – viz., those resulting from deliberation into specific 'whether *p*' questions – look as though they aim at *knowledge* (and so would be apt when *this* aim, the aim of believing *knowledgeably*, is aptly attained), it seems we must have gone wrong somewhere in our theory to this point. It is a theory that, thus far, is centred around the idea that all beliefs univocally 'aim' at truth. But *why* should beliefs be univocal in their aims (i.e., such that they always 'aim' only at success, never apt success) given that other performances (e.g., basketball shots) clearly aren't like this. And moreover, why should we stick to this idea when the examples given here suggest that not even *beliefs* are like this?

This is the crux of the *performance granularity problem*. Beliefs, like other performances, seem not to be *uniformly* ambitious in their aims across all contexts in which they are attempted. This observation lines up with what also seems to hold for all other kinds of aimed performances. Some aim constitutively at success any way, some aim intentionally at apt success, and *not* just at success any way.

Sosa seems to have noticed this problem soon after *Knowledge Full Well* (2010). His *Judgement and Agency* (2015) attempts an answer. The key new move is to not only stratify *knowledge* (as we've already done), but to *stratify our attempts at knowledge* – viz., our beliefs. Making this kind of move, though, amounts to more than just a cosmetic tweak. It requires revisiting with a critical eye what has, to this point, served as a kind of base-level axiom of the framework: viz., the idea that *any aimed performance* whatsoever (be it in epistemology or elsewhere) is apt only iff the *aim* that is internal to the performance type is attained through skill or ability.

Here's a question we've danced around so far: for a given aim, α, and a performance-type ϕ which has α as its internal or constitutive aim (and so which distinguishes ϕ as the type of performance it is), what *determines* that ϕ is α-aimed (rather than, say, β aimed)? Simple analogies to archery are compatible in principle with different answers. Moreover, guided just by the archery analogy and other sports analogies, simply acknowledging that performance-distinguishing aims are *constitutive* of the relevant performance types as opposed to non-constitutive also doesn't get us very far. Such an acknowledgement just pushes back the question further – viz., for a given constitutive aim, α, and a performance-type ϕ that has α as its constitutive aim, what *determines* that ϕ is constitutively α-aimed (rather than β-aimed?)?

Sosa's latest (2015 onwards) picture adds new clarity here by distinguishing between how aimed-performances are evaluable (with reference to AAA performance assessment) with reference to aims that are of two kinds (i) functional or teleological; and (ii) intentional; understanding the latter involves another important distinction. By getting this all on the table, we can then see how belief can be stratified in a principled way into two species – what Sosa terms 'functional beliefs' and 'judgemental beliefs'.

I'm now going to cover just the essential detail to understanding the difference, how the distinction resolves the performance granularity problem, and how it can be incorporated into our wider core triad.

With that in mind, let's look first at how an aimed performance (or, more generally, aimed attempts) can acquire the aims they have *teleologically*. A simple example from Sosa involves the state of alertness of a crouching cat: this state may be teleologically *aimed* at detecting vulnerable prey, simply because that state has acquired such a biological function (to detect prey when present), with reference to which we can explain (in the presence of prey) whether the alertness is successful or not as a state of alertness.[61] Apart from biological functions, social conventions can also determine teleological aims. It is social convention that fixes the teleological aim of an archery shot as that of hitting the target. That's why there is always a sense in which an archery shot, qua archery shot, is not successful if it misses the target, and regardless of what the archer thinks or intends while undertaking that performance.

When we make a given attempt, the 'aim' constitutive of the attempt might also be fixed in part by our intentions with respect to *how* the (e.g., functional/ teleological) aim is secured. Think again here of the basketball player whose shot at the hoop aims at aptness in a way that differs from how the novice chucking a wild shot hoping to win a bet is just hoping to get it in *any way*. The former is a shot aimed intentionally at apt success, even if also, at the same time, merely teleologically (with reference to social conventions that establish what counts as making a basket) at success. Such a shot, aimed intentionally at aptness, then, doesn't succeed relative to the aim of apt success even when the ball goes in, *if* it doesn't go in aptly, which is exactly what the shooter attempted with intention to do. (This observation lines up with our practices of praise/blame: the coach might criticise the player even when the shot goes in, if the shot was poorly selected (e.g., a half-court shot in the middle of the game[62]), taking on far too much risk than is warranted. Likewise, the judge reprimands the juror discovered to have arrived at the correct view without any deliberating of evidence but by guessing.)

We've already said enough to put on the table the core distinction between functional and judgemental beliefs, articulated with reference to functional/ teleological and intentional aims, respectively:

Functional belief: Aims (teleologically or functionally) at truth.

Judgemental belief: Aims (intentionally) at (first-order) aptness.[63]

The distinction between functional and judgemental beliefs marks two *different* kinds of performance. Success at the second kind of performance (an *aptness*-aimed attempt) asymmetrically entails success at the first kind of performance (a truth-aimed attempt). This is good news: a stratified picture of beliefs (with

---

[61] As Sosa notes, whether as a state it can count as a [sic. attempt] in any ordinary sense is hence irrelevant to our focus on [sic. attempts] that have an aim and to which we may then apply our AAA aim-involving normative account. See Sosa 2015, chapter 5, n. 5.

[62] Note, though, that a half-court shot might *not* incur criticism, as manifesting poor shot selection, if practical pressures warrant (unlike in the normal course of the game) taking inordinate risk.

[63] I am making a simplifying assumption here that these categories do not cut across each other.

judgemental beliefs aimed intentionally[64] *higher*, epistemically, than the former kind of belief) is just what was needed to respond to the central worry captured by the performance granularity problem.

And here is a connected point: notice that by distinguishing between truth-aimed and aptness-aimed species of beliefs, we are in a position to appreciate how 'high-grade' knowledge derives *from a distinctive kind of high-grade attempt* (an aptness-aimed attempt) rather than from a suitably connected concatenation of individual truth-aimed attempts at the first- and second-order, as was the case on the theory up to this point that replaced reflective knowledge with knowledge full well at the top of the hierarchy.

The working idea, then, will be to replace knowledge full well (as previously defined) with *fully apt judgement* at the top of our stratified knowledge hierarchy. Since in judging we aim intentionally at (first-order) aptness, judgement is *successful* just in case one's affirmation at the first order is *apt* and not merely true. But a *judgement* is itself *apt* iff *that aim distinctive of judgement* – the aim of first-order aptness – is *itself* aptly attained. This requires apt risk assessment that the affirmation (whether *p*) would likely enough be not just true but *apt*. And finally, a judgement is *fully apt* just when one's affirmation whether *p* is guided to aptness (and thus, to what it is that judgement aims at) *by* one's apt risk assessment. We'll return to this 'guided to aptness' point with a critical eye shortly. But for now, we're in a position to put the updated core triad in view.

Revised Core Triad (Stratified Virtue Epistemology)

- **Revised core knowledge thesis (CKT**)**: Propositional knowledge is apt belief, functional or judgemental.
- **Revised normative kind thesis (NKT**)**: Knowledge is a stratified normative kind, realised by stratified aimed attempts when apt. Functional (truth-aimed) beliefs when apt realise low-grade knowledge. Judgemental beliefs (aimed at low-grade *knowledge*) when apt realise high-grade knowledge.
- **Cognitive achievement thesis (CAT**)**: Knowledge is a (species of) stratified cognitive achievement, with a hierarchy of grades, with *fully apt judgement* at the top of the hierarchy.

3.2 Judgemental Knowledge 1: From Guidance to Basing

This section and the next motivate, and then develop, two new substantive additions (concerning guidance, and background conditions, respectively) to

---

[64] The idea that deliberative judgement is a species of intentional action is not new. See, along with Sosa, McHugh 2013; Peacocke 1998; Shah and Velleman 2006; and Soteriou 2013. Compare McGrath (in press).

the working picture so far. What we're going to look at now is, specifically, *guidance* – viz., what it is that (in cases of fully apt judgement) 'connects the levels'. Recall that a *fully apt* judgement requires that your aptness on the first order (i.e., affirming *p* aptly) be '*guided by* apt awareness on the second order' that the first-order affirmation would be apt (likely enough).

Just as your basketball shot falls short if your apt risk assessment at the second order (even if that risk assessment is apt) is performatively an idle wheel (i.e., doesn't guide you to first-order aptness – as would be the case if you decided whether to shoot by ignoring the apt risk assessment and flipping a coin), the same holds true in the case of judgement. A fully apt judgement requires that your aptness on the first order (i.e., affirming *p* aptly) be 'guided by apt awareness on the second order' that the first-order affirmation would be apt (likely enough).

So what exactly is meant by 'guided by'? Sosa takes this as a primitive. We know from examples (such as coin flipping cases) that guidance implies *at least* some kind of influence. Your risk assessment at the second-order needs to, in some way, inform or shape your performing aptly at the first-order. Otherwise such risk assessment would be ineffectual for the purposes of PERFORMANCE UPGRADE.

As we've already seen, the *output* of the risk assessment (of a fully apt judger) at the second order is just an item of knowledge: on the terminology introduced in the previous section: the output is *predictive reflective knowledge*. So, predictive reflective knowledge ought to suffice for playing the relevant *guidance* role in the theory, and in a way that will satisfy PERFORMANCE UPGRADE.

I want to now suggest that such knowledge is not quite built for this. My resolution to this problem, though, will not be to find something other than predictive reflective knowledge to play the guidance role, but rather, to replace 'guidance' with *basing* in our thinking about level connection.

So *why* can't predictive reflective knowledge suffice to 'guide' one to first-order aptness? Consider that what is necessary for 'settling' the question of whether to perform any action, ϕ, intentionally, will never be just the answer to a 'whether-*p*' question, but the answer to a *whether-to* question.

A whether-*p* question will always in principle be settled by belief (or knowledge), but plausibly the latter kind of 'whether-to' question is *settled* only when one forms an *intention* to ϕ. In this case, the relevant intention would be an intention to affirm or forbear. Simply *possessing* knowledge of a counterfactual (were one to affirm, one would do so aptly) of the sort that one has when one has predictive reflective knowledge accordingly *underdetermines* the matter of *whether to* form an intention to affirm. Some crucial ingredient is missing here. But what? Sosa leaves this unexplained. I'll now try to fill in the gap.

Notice that a missing part of this story seems to be that the second-order knowledge one has needs to somehow be explained to serve as *motivating* the agent to affirm when they go on to do so. A natural way to do this is to conceptualise the second-order predictive reflective knowledge (that one would affirm aptly, were one to affirm) as furnishing a *normative reason* for affirming rather than forbearing. As Maria Alvarez (2017) notes, we should expect any viable story about how normative reasons motivate any intentional action, judgemental or otherwise, to explain how one's having a normative reason for one to perform an intentional action, ϕ, can do two main things: (i) how it can motivate one to ϕ, and (ii) to ϕ *for* that reason (Alvarez 2017, section 2).

Accordingly, if we are going to vindicate the claim that predictive reflective knowledge (i.e., one's second-order apt awareness that their first-order affirmation whether p would likely enough be apt) is a *normative reason* for affirming that p, then we'd need some story for why a thinker *for whom this is a normative reason to affirm would be capable of being motivated to affirm for that normative reason.*

One 'shortcut' for securing this result would be to throw all-in with a strong Humean theory of normative reasons, according to which something is a normative reason for S to ϕ only if S has a desire that would be served by their ϕ-ing. Part and parcel with this idea is that normative reasons, given their connection with desires, are intrinsically motivating – viz., what is called 'reasons internalism'. The Humean theory of reasons, and 'reasons internalism', which is closely associated with it, are both controversial. Fortunately, there is a way to get everything we want without needing to appeal to any thesis that applies to all normative reasons for action *as such*.

Regardless of whether all normative reasons bear any essential connection with motivation – this is where a lot of the quibbling lies – we can still offer a relatively straightforward explanation for how a thinker's predictive reflective knowledge could constitute a normative reason for them to affirm when they do; we do this by appealing to a feature distinctive of judgement's being deliberative and intentional rather than merely implicit in the first place – viz., to a judger's *intentional aim to affirm if and only if doing so would be (first-order) apt*. Because, in judging, one is *already* intentionally aiming at aptness in this way, we can make sense of how one's predictive reflective knowledge (when *combined* with their intentional aim to affirm iff apt at the first-order) would have the capacity to motivate them to affirm *for this reason*.

Of course, I say 'capable' because one might possess a good normative reason to ϕ while failing to actually base one's ϕ-ing on the good normative reason one has – where the basing relation (in the case of intentional action) holds between a reason and an action if and only if the reason is a reason *for which* the action is performed. When a judgement is fully apt – and the knowledge one has at the second order (that one's affirmation would be first-order apt) is capable of genuinely increasing the quality of one's performance in affirming whether *p* – we should unpack our thinking about level connection in terms of one's *basing* one's apt affirmation at the first-order *on the output (predictive reflective knowledge) of one's apt risk assessment at the second-order* that one's first-order affirmation would likely enough be apt. This is an instance of upgrading performance quality by basing the performance on a good normative reason one has.

In sum, the basing-centred conceptualisation of the kind of level connection that should characterise the structure of fully apt judgement has important advantages over the guidance view we find in Sosa. It demystifies how counter-factual knowledge would be *motivating* in such a way as to influence one's affirming (rather than forbearing) at the first order. And – by assimilating predictive reflective knowledge to the status of a normative reason for intentionally affirming – we offer a clear story of how that 'influence' would have what it takes to boost the quality of the performance. The boost comes from the performance being based on the good normative reason to affirm supplied by the apt risk assessment in conjunction with the intentional aim to affirm iff doing so would be apt.

3.3 Judgemental Knowledge 2: Background Conditions and De Minimis Risk

The stratified picture I've been going in for has so far charted different directions from Sosa on two points: (i) how to think of the place of reflective knowledge within a stratified virtue epistemology, and (ii) how to conceive of the structure of level connection as it features in an account of fully apt judgement. Both revisions, we've seen, give the wider view extra explanatory power and plausibility. In this final section, I want to carve out one further substantive development, which will be to replace Sosa's account of *background conditions*, as this features in his theory of fully apt judgement, with an account of *de minimis risk*.[65]

We haven't discussed 'background conditions' yet. Sosa's view on this score, I think, represents his attempt to engage with one of the most fascinating parts of a stratified virtue epistemology. In this respect, we're saving the best for last.

---

[65] This section draws from ideas first developed in an article for *Philosophical Quarterly* (see Carter 2021b).

In order to get Sosa's theory of background conditions on the table, let's consider a very simple case. Suppose a basketball player is about to shoot a free throw inside a well-lit arena at night-time. *Unbeknownst to the shooter*, a beaver is chewing on a wire outside the arena, and the deterioration of that wire easily could cause the lights in the arena to go completely dark, right as the player is about to shoot. Fortunately, the beaver gets distracted and quits chewing the wire just in time. The shot goes in.

Compare now with an inquirer: having weighed the evidence carefully, a thinker is in the process of affirming judgementally on the matter of whether *p. Unbeknownst* to the inquirer, a maniac on the other side of the world with a bomb is deciding whether to destroy the world, and decides by flipping a coin.[66] Fortunately, it was heads: the world is not destroyed. The inquirer then makes their judgement that *p*.

In each case, something easily could have happened that would have 'spoiled' the relevant performance. But it's not obvious (in the former case) that the player's shot was any worse quality – when it goes in – on account of simply assuming the lights would stay on and getting lucky about that. And likewise for the inquirer: the judgement's quality qua judgement doesn't seem to be downgraded by the inquirer's obliviousness to the maniac on the other side of the world. In each case, the performance seems to be beholden to luck, but not *credit-reducing* luck.

Sympathetic to such observations, Sosa embraces a distinction within the class of things that could cause a performance to fail, between

(i) the kinds of things a fully apt performer must heed in order to safeguard against credit-reducing luck; and

(ii) the kinds of things they are free to non-negligently assume are already in place.

Let's look at the first category. As Sosa (2017) puts it, an athlete, in order to meet the predictive reflective knowledge condition on fully apt performance 'needs to consider various shape and situation factors: how tired he is, for example, how far from the target, and so on, for the many shape and situation factors that can affect performance' (191).

As for Category (ii):

> But there are many factors that he need not heed. It is no concern of an athlete as such whether an earthquake might hit, or a flash tornado, or a hydrogen bomb set off by a maniac leader of a rogue state, and so on. As an athlete, he is not negligent for ignoring such factors. (191)

---

[66] For discussion of this example, see Sosa 2017, 216.

Such things are of 'no concern' to the athlete, as such, *even though* earthquakes, tornadoes, bombs – as well as electricity failures – are the sort of things that could (obviously) spoil a performance if they in fact materialised.

Category (ii) – viz., the kinds of things an apt performer can *non-negligently* assume are already in place – corresponds to what Sosa calls 'background conditions'. We can identify background conditions, on Sosa's view (for a given performance), by investigating what is entailed by the presence of pertinent seat, shape, and situation conditions.

This looks initially like a recipe that will secure, intuitively, the right result in both the athletic and judgemental performance examples here. In the former: the situational component of a basketball competence includes normal lighting conditions, and the presence of such conditions entails the existence of some light source. Thus, the obtaining of a light source, as the thought goes, is something a shooter can non-negligently assume to be in place while performing with full aptness. In the latter case, the same rationale holds, except that (as the bomb is an extreme example) the existence of the world that would be threatened by such a bomb is entailed by the presence of the situational as well as the seat and shape components of any judgemental competence. In this respect *that the world will remain in place (throughout the performance)* is background condition thrice over. And so, qua background condition, if the obtaining of the world happened to itself be rendered unsafe by the nearness of the bomb scenario, this isn't enough to implicate credit-reducing luck to the performance on the theory of background conditions Sosa prefers.

Sosa is right to observe that any performance, in any domain of endeavour (epistemic, athletic, or otherwise) will be such that we should expect that there will be *some things* the obtaining of which can non-negligently be assumed to be in place such that when such things obtain only unsafely this wouldn't implicate any credit-reducing luck.

That said, Sosa's specification of background conditions faces a problem[67]: it doesn't screen off possible *overlap* between (i) what's entailed by the presence of the pertinent seat, shape, and situation conditions; and (ii) risks to the seat, shape, and situational conditions themselves, the safety of which a fully apt performer must competently monitor.

In the remainder of this section, I'll first explain the problem, and then show how to fix it with some additional theory.

---

[67] See, for example, Carter 2021b.

3.3.1 The Overlap Problem

Consider an example case: take the presence of normal atmospheric pressure in one's environment. The obtaining of normal atmospheric conditions is going to get ruled in as a background condition on Sosa's entailment-based criteria for almost *any* athletic performance-type, as one cannot be in proper shape without ambient atmospheric pressure, itself a necessary condition for the presence of breathable oxygen. As such, it ought to be by Sosa's lights that a basketball player could shoot fully aptly *while ignoring threats to the obtaining of normal atmospheric pressure* – even when such threats are modally close.

But – and here's where the worry comes into view – dips in atmospheric pressure are well-known to also lead to one's *shape* being compromised (e.g., by causing joint stiffness). Notice that when thinking about atmospheric pressure in *this* way, it looks as though a fully apt performer could non-negligently ignore nearby threats to normal levels of atmospheric pressure *only if* they can also non-negligently ignore more mundane threats to being in proper shape (e.g., tiredness). But these are exactly the kinds of things Sosa takes it that a fully apt performer can't (in assessing risks to the first-order aptness of a performance) be oblivious to.

It looks, then, like Sosa's view allows problematic overlap: the obtaining of certain conditions gets ruled in as background conditions even while, by the lights of the theory, remaining such that one would need to take them into account as part of the kind of risk assessment that full aptness requires.

3.3.2 A Solution: Full Aptness and De Minimis Risk

A solution to the problem will need to do the following: it will need to cleanly separate what we described earlier as Category 1 and Category 2 conditions – viz., between (i) the kinds of things a fully apt performer must heed in order to safeguard against credit-reducing luck; and (ii) the kinds of things a fully apt performer is free to non-negligently assume are already in place. More concisely: a solution needs to screen off the possibility of 'overlap' between Category 1 and Category 2.

Here's the core idea that I think can help us to avoid overlap. We'll look at the idea in the case of performances generally, and then apply it more specifically to the case of fully apt judgement specifically.

The general idea I want to propose (as a replacement for Sosa's theory of background conditions) is the following:

(†) A fully apt performer can non-negligently ignore risks to the aptness of a given performance type-ϕ if and only if the risks count as *de minimis* with reference to rules with *reproduction value* for ϕ-type performances.

This view introduces a few new elements – including the idea of *reproduction value* into the framework, which (as well see) is going to be the key idea for making sense of de minimis risk. Let's take these ideas in turn.

First, reproduction value. This is a concept that is tied to a more fundamental idea, that of *practice sustaining rules*. Let's define generally – in a way that abstracts from athletic and epistemic domains – a 'practice' as a way of doing things and a 'rule' as a prescriptive principle or standard of conduct. Rules are important to practices: they 'hold practices together'. But how do they do this? A straightforward and plausible recent answer has been defended by John Turri (2017), one that is value driven:

Practice-sustaining rules: A rule normatively sustains a practice if and only if the value achieved by following the rule explains why agents continue following that rule.

'Don't break promises' counts as a sustaining rule for many kinds of practices: the value achieved by following this rule explains why clergy as well as bankers continue to follow it. Yelling 'bingo' if and only if you have a bingo is a practice-sustaining rule just for bingo: the value of doing this explains why players of bingo keep doing this. A practice might have many rules, though only some of these play the role of sustaining it, by leading to 'reproduction via value produced' – alternatively, by having *reproduction value.*

Many practices include *performances*. They do so when performances are prescribed, in certain conditions, by rules that sustain the practice. For example, the practice of archery includes the performance of shooting an arrow at a target. The practice of playing chess includes the performance of castling to defend the king. The practice of inquiry includes judgement, withholding, and so on.

For performances within any practice, one might try to take steps to safeguard against risks that that performance would be inapt. Let's return to our initial example of the night-time basketball player. One *could* do things to safeguard against the risk that the lights would go out and spoil a shot. One could adjust one's shooting technique slightly (perhaps gripping the ball more tightly) so that they can pull back more easily at the last moment. Although doing this would surely help to safeguard one against the risk to the inaptness of a would-be shot posed by the possibility that the lights would go out, following *that rule* (i.e., shoot in ways that are suitably risk averse vis-à-vis the scenario where the lights go out) is not a rule with *reproduction value* in basketball. There is *disvalue* within the practice of basketball to adhering to such a rule, and such disvalue would explain why following is not sustaining of that practice.

We've now got the core ideas in view with reference to which we can make sense of the normative idea of a risk to the aptness of a performance being *de minimis*, such that a fully apt performer can then non-negligently ignore it, as per (†). The phrase *de minimis* derives from the Latin sentence *de minimis non curat lex*, which translates (roughly) to 'The law should not concern itself with trifles' (e.g. the crime of stealing a penny). In decision theory, risks are termed de minimis risks whenever they are judged to be so 'small' that they should be *ignored*.

My suggestion for linking a de minimis proviso to rules with reproduction value is the following: a risk, R, to the aptness of a given performance, ϕ, is *de minimis*, *vis-à-vis* ϕ-ing, if and only if the safety of S's ϕ-ing against R can't be easily increased through adherence to one or more rules with reproduction value for ϕ-type performances. The safety of a performance against a risk concerns how easily the risk would materialise. Doing something to increase the safety of a performance against a risk is to do something that makes it less easy (holding fixed that you've done that thing) that the risk will materialise – viz., that, holding fixed that you've done that thing, the risk event materialises in further-out worlds than before. Unpacked more fully now, the original proposal (making the de minimis proviso explicit) can be read as follows: A fully apt performer can non-negligently ignore a risk R to the aptness of a given performance-type, ϕ, if and only if the safety of S's ϕ-ing against the R can't be easily increased through adherence to one or more rules with reproduction value for ϕ-type performances.

Let's see now how this view will get us the results we want, first by looking at two easy case pairs, and then at the kind of 'hard' case that seemed (for Sosa's view) to generate the overlap problem.

First, let's consider easy Category 1 cases (athletic and epistemic variations). In the athletic variation (V1) suppose Steph catches the ball and decides whether a particular shot is worth taking. From that distance and in his present tired condition, he is barely within his threshold for sufficient reliability. Oblivious to his tiredness he shoots anyway and makes it aptly. For the epistemic analogue (V2 of a Category 1 case) Steph* is birdwatching (in non-ideal lighting conditions) and is assessing whether a particular bird from fifty metres away is a goldfinch or a chaffinch. From that distance and in those conditions, he is barely within his threshold for sufficient reliability. Oblivious to the way the lighting conditions at that distance are nearly aptness impeding, Steph* judges (aptly) that it is a chaffinch.

Both of these cases feature performances that are first-order apt but not fully apt, and not fully apt because of defective second-order risk assessment: in neither case is the relevant (predictive reflective knowledge) required for full aptness present. That said, the view I've suggested would be in trouble if it ruled that monitoring for the relevant risks to aptness in *these* Category 1 cases would

.

qualify as de minimis. The good news is that the view does not generate that
(overly permissive) result. In V1, monitoring for how tiredness affects the limits
of one's shooting competence has reproduction value in basketball, and Steph
could easily increase his safety against the tiredness risk by monitoring for that;
the risk is thus *not* de minimis. And similar reasoning applies mutatis mutandis
for V2: monitoring for how lighting conditions affects the limits of one's visual-
perceptual competence (especially when such conditions aren't ideal) is
a valuable rule to follow within a practice (like bird-watching) where reliable
bird-spotting is valued, just as it will be valuable within our visual perceptual
practices (affected by lighting conditions) more generally. In sum: the proposal
doesn't problematically rule as de minimis risks that clearly fall into Category 1
(and are such a fully apt performer can't non-negligently disregard them).

To find two easy Category 2 cases (an athletic and an epistemic analogue), we
need to look no further than the case pair we used to kick off discussion in this
section. In V1, Steph shoots a basket while oblivious to the risk that the power in
the gymnasium could go out mid-shot, which it easily could have. In V2, the
inquirer is about to judge whether p, oblivious to the maniac with the bomb
flipping a coin whether to destroy the world, trivially spoiling all intellectual
performances. Like Category 1 cases, Category 2 cases feature risks to aptness
of the relevant performance. And the proposal I've suggested gets the right
result in both cases: in cases, the relevant risks will count as de minimis – given
that in *neither* case can safety against the relevant risk of inaptness be increased
by adherence to any rule with reproduction value. We already considered why
this would be so in V1 of our Category 2 case. The same holds in the epistemic
variation: monitoring for bomb-style risks lacks reproduction value in nearly
any kind of context of inquiry.

Let's transition now to the kind of 'overlap'-style case that posed a problem
for Sosa's view, and consider now how the proposed alternative view enjoys an
advantage. The case featured there (in the context of a basketball performance)
concerned risk of sudden changes in atmospheric pressure that could impede
one's shape (e.g., by causing joint stiffness, etc). We saw that Sosa's view seems
to classify this case as overlapping, problematically, in both Category 1 *and*
(because the obtaining of normal atmospheric conditions gets ruled in as
a background condition for basketball performance on his view) Category 2.
My suggested revision, on the other hand, gets the unambiguous result that the
case is Category 2 – the right result. The reason is that monitoring for atmospheric pressure dips will count as a de minimis risk to the aptness of a basketball
performance on my view. Granted, one *could* easily safeguard against that
particular risk by, say, carrying around an atmospheric barometer on the court.
But that doesn't matter for my proposal; this is because even so one can't

safeguard against this kind of risk by acting in accordance with any rules with basketball-relevant reproduction value. Thus, the risk is de minimis.

And what goes for basketball goes for performances generally, as well as for judgemental performances. Many inquiries will presumably have the same kind of rules with reproduction value – which is why safeguarding against risk of inaptness by, say, quadruple-checking results and doubly corroborating all testimony lack reproduction value in individual (and social) inquiry.

That said, the matter of what rules have reproduction value in *inquiry* will of course vary according to different contexts of inquiry, just as we should expect. Consider, for example, a homeowner and a fire officer judging what caused a given house fire. The homeowner might affirm aptly that the house was caused by faulty wiring, indeed the homeowner might judge *fully aptly*, on the basis of the fire officer's reliable expert testimony. The second-order risk assessment (pertinent to one's competence in receiving reliable testimony) needn't include monitoring for cleverly disguised tampering at the scene; one could of course double check the expert's testimony by investigating the scene themselves (and less competently so) – but such risks come out as de minimis vis-à-vis the first-order aptness of a competence in receiving expert testimony. (After all, no such first-order competence (at ascertaining the scene) is needed at all for one to know fully aptly on the word of the fire officer.) By contrast, fire officer's fully apt judgement will be different. The first-order competences exercised in making the judgement first-hand will include an assessment of the scene; aptly assessing for risks to the aptness of *that* kind of first-order assessment will include investigating difficult-to-spot signs of arson. Double-checking for deception – in the case of this kind of judgement – has reproduction value in the context of *expert* inquiry; the value of double-checking for arson explains why experts giving their judgements (but not testimonial receivers) will continue to do this. The risk, for the expert then, is *not* de minimis, even though technically the expert is affirming the same 'whether *p*' question as the novice testimonial recipient; they are doing so by way of different judgemental performances in inquiry.

In sum, then, my suggested replacement proposal *agrees* with Sosa that an account of full aptness needs to distinguish between Category 1 and 2 cases. He has offered his preferred strategy for doing this, by appealing to background conditions. I have shown that the criteria for satisfying Sosa-style background conditions generates overlap between Category 1 and Category 2. I've proposed an alternative way for distinguishing Category 2 cases from Category 1 cases (where a fully apt performer can ignore risks to inaptness of a performance) by taking them to track not background conditions but rather conditions captured by our view of *de minimis* risk. Rather than to say that a fully apt performer can ignore at the risks of inaptness when such risks are to the obtaining of background conditions (whatever conditions are entailed by the obtaining of the SSS of the relevant competence), I've defended here instead that a fully apt performer can non-negligently ignore risks to the aptness of a given performance type ϕ if and only if such risks count as de minimis with reference to rules with *reproduction value* for ϕ-type performances. This view was shown to get the benefits of Sosa's approach, while at the same time screening off problematic overlap.

3.4 Concluding Remarks

This section has moved the debate forward by offering a different take on the 'top of the hill' of our stratified virtue epistemology: fully apt judgement. We began by seeing how our working account of stratified knowledge best accommodates the performance granularity problem by signing up to a stratified picture of *belief* along the lines Sosa has suggested in his most recent epistemology, which distinguishes between functional and judgemental belief. We've then seen how the *structure* of the highest grade of knowledge – fully apt judgement – gets unpacked on Sosa's preferred picture, and we've made two substantive revisions to this structure. First, we replaced his 'guidance' approach to level connection with a 'basing' approach. Second, we replaced his theory of background conditions (as part of his wider view of what a fully apt performer can non-negligently ignore) with a theory of (performance-indexed) de minimis risk. In both cases, these substantive amendments have been added to avoid problems that faced the original proposal.

The end result, then, is a version of virtue epistemology that takes a lot of what allows Sosa's view to deliver the results it is shown to deliver (in Sections 1 and 2) but with extra improvements – all of which we've seen pertain to high-grade knowledge. We've (in Section 2) developed a new way of thinking about the place of reflective knowledge (and its different theoretical roles) in a stratified virtue epistemology, and then (in Section 3) we paired these updates with an upgraded view of fully apt judgement. As with any epistemology that does away with parts of orthodoxy (in our case, giving up the assumption that knowledge is uni-level), there are costs to pay. *Stratifying* our epistemology seems to risk such a cost (even if not the kinds of costs Kornblith had thought). I hope to have shown, first in Section 1 (at the first level), and then in the Sections 2 and 3) at the higher levels that stratified virtue epistemology of the sort outlined and defended here is very much worth its price.

References

Alvarez, Maria. 2017. 'Reasons for Action: Justification, Motivation, Explanation.' In *The Stanford Encyclopedia of Philosophy*, edited by Edward N. Zalta, Winter. https://plato.stanford.edu/entries/reasons-just-vs-expl/.

Ball, Brian. 2013. 'Knowledge Is Normal Belief'. *Analysis* 73 (1): 69–76.

Baumann, Peter. 2014. 'No Luck with Knowledge? On a Dogma of Epistemology'. *Philosophy and Phenomenological Research* 89 (3): 523–51.

Bird, Alexander, and Emma Tobin. 2022. 'Natural Kinds'. https://plato.stan ford.edu/entries/natural-kinds/.

Carter, J. Adam. 2021a. 'Exercising Abilities'. *Synthese* 198: 2495–509.

Carter, J. Adam. 2021b. 'De Minimis Normativism: A New Theory of Full Aptness'. *The Philosophical Quarterly* 71 (1): 16–36. https://doi.org/10.1093/pq/pqaa017.

Carter, J. Adam. 2016. 'Metaepistemology and Relativism'. In *Metaepistemology and Relativism*, 212–32. Springer.

2023. *A Telic Theory of Trust*. Oxford University Press.

Carter, J. Adam, and Benjamin Jarvis. 2012. 'Against Swamping'. *Analysis* 72 (4): 690–99. https://doi.org/10.1093/analys/ans118.

Carter, J. Adam, and Robin McKenna. 2019. 'Kornblith versus Sosa on Grades of Knowledge'. *Synthese* 196 (12): 4989–5007. https://doi.org/10.1007/s11229-018-1689-8.

Carter, J. Adam, Duncan Pritchard, and John Turri. 2018. 'The Value of Knowledge'. In *Stanford Encyclopedia of Philosophy*, edited by Edward N. Zalta, Winter. https://plato.stanford.edu/entries/knowledge-value/.

Carter, J. Adam and Robert Cowan. 2023. 'Safety and Dream Scepticism in Sosa's Epistemology' (ms.).

Carter, J. Adam, and Ernest Sosa. 2021. 'Metaepistemology'. In *Stanford Encyclopedia of Philosophy*, edited by Edward N. Zalta, Winter. https://plato.stanford.edu/entries/metaepistemology/.

Cassam, Quassim. 2009. 'What Is Knowledge?' *Royal Institute of Philosophy Supplements* 64: 101–20.

Chisholm, Roderick M. 1977. *Theory of Knowledge*. Prentice Hall.

Colaço, David, Wesley Buckwalter, Stephen Stich, and Edouard Machery. 2014. 'Epistemic Intuitions in Fake-Barn Thought Experiments'. *Episteme* 11 (2): 199–212.

Cottingham, John. 2002. 'Descartes and the Voluntariness of Belief'. *The Monist* 85 (3): 343–60.

Drayson, Zoe. 2014. 'The Personal/Subpersonal Distinction'. *Philosophy Compass* 9 (5): 338–46. https://doi.org/10.1111/phc3.12124.

Gagne, Robert M., and Ernest C. Smith Jr. 1962. 'A Study of the Effects of Verbalization on Problem Solving'. *Journal of Experimental Psychology* 63 (1): 12–18.

Gerken, Mikkel. 2018. 'Against Knowledge-First Epistemology'. In *Knowledge First: Approaches in Epistemology and Mind*, edited by J. Adam Carter, Emma Gordon and Benjamin W. Jarvis, 46–71. Oxford University Press.

Goldberg, Sanford. 2023. 'A Novel Process Reliabilist Response to the Swamping Problem'. *Analysis*. https://doi.org/10.1093/analys/anac062.

Goldman, Alvin. 1967. 'A Causal Theory of Knowing'. *The Journal of Philosophy* 64 (12): 357–72.

1999. *Knowledge in a Social World*. Oxford University Press.

2009. 'Williamson on Knowledge and Evidence'. In *Williamson on Knowledge*, edited by Patrick Greenough, Duncan Pritchard, and Timothy Williamson, 73–91. Oxford University Press.

Greco, John. 2008. 'What's Wrong with Contextualism?' *The Philosophical Quarterly*, 58 (232): 416–36.

Greco, John. 2010. *Achieving Knowledge: A Virtue-Theoretic Account of Epistemic Normativity*. Cambridge University Press.

2020a. 'Safety in Sosa'. *Synthese* 197 (12): 5147–57. https://doi.org/10.1007/s11229-018-1863-z.

2020b. *Transmitting Knowledge*. Cambridge University Press.

Henderson, David K., and John Greco. 2015. *Epistemic Evaluation: Purposeful Epistemology*. Oxford University PressOxford .

Hetherington, Stephen. 1998. 'Actually Knowing'. *The Philosophical Quarterly (1950–)* 48 (193): 453–69.

2001. *Good Knowledge, Bad Knowledge: On Two Dogmas of Epistemology*. Oxford University Press.

2011. *How to Know: A Practicalist Conception of Knowledge*. Wiley-Blackwell.

2013. 'Knowledge Can Be Lucky'. *Contemporary Debates in Epistemology* 2: 164–76.

2016. *Knowledge and the Gettier Problem*. Cambridge University Press.

2018. 'The Redundancy Problem: From Knowledge-Infallibilism to Knowledge-Minimalism', *Synthese* 195: 4683–702.

Ichikawa, Jonathan. 2009. 'Dreaming and Imagination'. *Mind & Language* 24 (1): 103–21.

Kallestrup, Jesper, and Duncan Pritchard. 2012. 'Robust Virtue Epistemology and Epistemic Anti-Individualism'. *Pacific Philosophical Quarterly* 93 (1): 84–103.

Kornblith, Hilary. 2004. 'Sosa on Human and Animal Knowledge'. In *Ernest Sosa and His Critics*, edited by John Greco, 126–34. Blackwell.

———. 2012. *On Reflection*. Oxford University Press.

Kvanvig, Jonathan L. 2003. *The Value of Knowledge and the Pursuit of Understanding*. Cambridge University Press.

Lackey, Jennifer. 2007. 'Why We Don't Deserve Credit for Everything We Know'. *Synthese* 158 (3): 345–61.

———. 2009. 'Knowledge and Credit'. *Philosophical Studies* 142: 27–42.

Lederman, Harvey. 2022. 'The Introspective Model of Genuine Knowledge in Wang Yangming'. *Philosophical Review* 131 (2): 169–213.

Littlejohn, Clayton, and J. Adam Carter. 2021. *This Is Epistemology*. John Wiley & Sons.

McGrath, Matthew. 2022. 'A Limitation on Agency in Judgment'. *Synthese* 200. https://doi.org/10.1007/s11229-022-03616-y.

Melchior, Guido. 2019. *Knowing and Checking: An Epistemological Investigation*. Routledge.

Miracchi, Lisa. 2017. 'Perception First'. *The Journal of Philosophy* 114 (12): 629–77.

Miracchi, Lisa, and J. Adam Carter. 2022. 'Refitting the Mirrors: On Structural Analogies in Epistemology and Action Theory'. *Synthese*. https://doi.org/10.1007/s11229-022-03462-y.

Nozick, Robert. 1981. *Philosophical Investigations*. Belknap Press of Harvard University.

Olsson, Erik J. 2007. 'Reliabilism, Stability, and the Value of Knowledge'. *American Philosophical Quarterly* 44 (4): 343–55.

Otero, Manuel Pérez. 2020. 'Williamson on Defining Knowledge'. *Episteme*, July, 1–17. https://doi.org/10.1017/epi.2020.27.

Perrine, Timothy. 2014. 'Against Kornblith Against Reflective Knowledge'. *Logos & Episteme* 5 (3): 351–60.

Pritchard, Duncan. 2023. 'Moderate Knowledge Externalism'. In *Externalism About Knowledge*, edited by L. R. G. Oliveira, 131–49. Oxford University Press.

———. 2005. *Epistemic Luck*. Clarendon Press.

———. 2007. 'Anti-Luck Epistemology'. *Synthese* 158 (3): 277–97.

2009. 'The Value of Knowledge'. *The Harvard Review of Philosophy* 16 (1): 86–103. https://doi.org/10.5840/harvardreview20091616.

2012. 'Anti-Luck Virtue Epistemology'. *The Journal of Philosophy* 109 (3): 247–79.

2015. 'Anti-Luck Epistemology and the Gettier Problem'. *Philosophical Studies* 172 (1): 93–111.

2016. 'Epistemic Risk'. *The Journal of Philosophy* 113 (11): 550–71.

Rabinowicz, Wlodek, and Rønnow-Rasmussen, Toni. 2000. 'A Distinction in Value: Intrinsic and for Its Own Sake'. *Proceedings of the Aristotelian Society* 100 (1): 33–51.

Reed, Baron. 2002. 'How to Think about Fallibilism'. *Philosophical Studies* 107 (2): 143–57.

Shope, Robert K. 1983. *The Analysis of Knowing: A Decade of Research*: Princeton University Press.

Smithies, Declan. 2011. 'Attention Is Rational-Access Consciousness'. In *Attention: Philosophical and Psychological Essays*, edited by Christopher Mole, Declan Smithies, and Wayne Wu, 247–73. Oxford University Press.

Sosa, Ernest. 1980. 'The Raft and the Pyramid: Coherence versus Foundations in the Theory of Knowledge'. *Midwest Studies in Philosophy* 5: 3–25.

1991. *Knowledge in Perspective: Selected Essays in Epistemology*. Cambridge University Press.

1997. 'Reflective Knowledge in the Best Circles'. *Journal of Philosophy* 94 (8): 410–30. https://doi.org/jphil199794827.

2007. *A Virtue Epistemology: Apt Belief and Reflective Knowledge*, vol 1. Oxford University Press.

2009. *Reflective Knowledge: Apt Belief and Reflective Knowledge*, vol. 2. Oxford University Press.

2010a. 'How Competence Matters in Epistemology'. *Philosophical Perspectives* 24 (1): 465–75.

2010b. *Knowing Full Well*. Princeton University Press.

2015. *Judgment & Agency*. Oxford University Press.

2017. *Epistemology*. Princeton: Princeton University Press.

2021. *Epistemic Explanations: A Theory of Telic Normativity, and What It Explains*. Oxford University Press.

Swain, Marshall. 1981. *Reasons and Knowledge*. Cornell University Press.

Turri, John. 2016. 'Knowledge Judgments in "Gettier" Cases'. *A Companion to Experimental Philosophy*, 337–48.

Turri, John, Wesley Buckwalter, and Peter Blouw. 2015. 'Knowledge and Luck'. *Psychonomic Bulletin & Review* 22: 378–90.

2017. 'Sustaining Rules: A Model and Application'. In *Knowledge First: Approaches in Epistemology and Mind*, edited by J. Adam Carter, Emma C. Gordon, and Benjamin Jarvis, 259–77. Oxford University Press.

Williamson, Timothy. 2000. *Knowledge and Its Limits*. Oxford University Press.

2005. 'Précis of Knowledge and Its Limits 1'. *Philosophy and Phenomenological Research* 70 (2): 431–35.

Zagzebski, Linda. 2003. 'The Search for the Source of Epistemic Good'. *Metaphilosophy* 34 (1–2): 12–28.

Zagzebski, Linda T. 1996. *Virtues of the Mind: An Inquiry into the Nature of Virtue and the Ethical Foundations of Knowledge*. Cambridge University Press.

Cambridge Elements

Epistemology

Stephen Hetherington
University of New South Wales, Sydney

Stephen Hetherington is Professor Emeritus of Philosophy at the University of New South Wales, Sydney. He is the author of numerous books, including *Knowledge and the Gettier Problem* (Cambridge University Press, 2016) and *What Is Epistemology?* (Polity, 2019), and is the editor of several others, including *Knowledge in Contemporary Epistemology* (with Markos Valaris: Bloomsbury, 2019) and *What the Ancients Offer to Contemporary Epistemology* (with Nicholas D. Smith: Routledge, 2020). He was the Editor-in-Chief of the *Australasian Journal of Philosophy* from 2013 until 2022.

About the Series
This Elements series seeks to cover all aspects of a rapidly evolving field, including emerging and evolving topics such as: fallibilism; knowinghow; self-knowledge; knowledge of morality; knowledge and injustice; formal epistemology; knowledge and religion; scientific knowledge; collective epistemology; applied epistemology; virtue epistemology; wisdom. The series demonstrates the liveliness and diversity of the field, while also pointing to new areas of investigation.

Cambridge Elements ☰

Epistemology

Elements in the Series

Printed in the United States
by Baker & Taylor Publisher Services